like a house **on fire**

Other books by Steve Scott

Crying for a Vision
Boundaries I: Asian Afterimages (poetry)
Boundaries II: The St. Petersburg Fragments (poetry)

like a house

on fire

Renewal of
the Arts in a
Postmodern
Culture

Steve
Scott

Wipf and Stock Publishers
EUGENE, OREGON

Wipf and Stock Publishers
199 West 8th Avenue, Suite 3
Eugene, Oregon 97401

Like a House on Fire
Renewal of the Arts in a Postmodern Culture
By Scott, Steve
Copyright© January, 1997 Scott, Steve
ISBN: 1-59244-114-9
Publication date: December, 2002
Previously published by Cornerstone Press Chicago, January, 1997 .

CONTENTS

PREFACE

I MADE a commitment to Christ in the late sixties; even then the call for discernment in the world of popular culture and a call to excellence in the arts was being sounded throughout the Church. Francis Schaeffer and Hans Rookmaaker, influential writers in the subject of Christianity and the arts, were receiving wide attention. The Arts Centre Group in London was growing from the dream of a few into a concrete reality; it would serve as a basis to nurture, support and offer critical reflection for many artists and thinkers in the years to follow. With the emergence of the Jesus Movement in the United States came fresh and relevant cultural expressions that reached a hand out to the neighbor while keeping both feet on the Rock.

As the countercultural music expressions of the late sixties and early seventies ossified into today's "business as usual" contemporary Christian music scene, there was a steady growth of interest in the arts in the Church. Conferences, books and exhibits explored everything from the roots of creativity to the myriad surfaces of contemporary culture. From Washington, D.C. in the States to Denpasar in Bali, Indonesia, artists and thinkers gathered to share, learn, and experience God's presence in the creative genres. The first East-West Christian Arts Festival took place in St.

Petersburg, Russia in 1992; it was there I began reflecting on the current and future state of the arts in the Church. I believe that as we enter the next millennium Christian artists and their work will gain greater exposure and prominence. Now, more than ever, we need to attend to matters that prevent us from thinking and doing our best.

This book began life as a series of essays, lectures and Bible studies. Accordingly, I first thank all the people and publications who made these materials available in their original form. Secondly, I would like to thank Pat Peterson for his tremendously hard work in helping shape this material into book form. I would also like to thank Warehouse Christian Ministries, Sacramento, for faithfully continuing to keep their foot in the door of the arts. Lastly, I am grateful to the many artists I have met at the conferences in Bali and elsewhere who continue to be an inspiration and a light to the path.

STEVE SCOTT

like a house **on fire**

INTRODUCTION

> The question of whether or not art will change the
> world is not a relevant question anymore. The world is
> changing already, in inescapable ways. We can no longer
> deny the evidence at hand. The need to transform the
> egocentric vision that is encoded in our entire world
> view is the crucial task that lies ahead for our culture.
> The issue is whether art will rise to the occasion and
> make itself useful to all that is going on.[1]

AFTER observing the tremendous progress of Christians in
the arts over the last twenty years, I still find many
paralyzed in their thinking about creativity and iron their
practice of creativity. Of course, they can talk the talk about
the need for excellence. They have the terminology of the
idiom down pat, yet are not moving. There is need for
renewal, for reviving, of the arts in the West, and an
integration of the arts with life and the surrounding culture.

Travels in India, South East Asia, Indonesia and Russia
have shown me clearly that spirituality and cultural
expression can be woven together. In Bali and Java there are
dedicated workers who are taking traditional art forms such
as dance and puppetry, and investing them with Christian
intention and value in the face of a culture rooted in

1. Suzi Gablik, *The Reenchantment of Art* (New York: Thames & Hudson, 1992),
p. 141.

animistic and Hindu beliefs. In Russia, I saw biblically-inspired artwork of the highest quality in several museums. This work had been preserved by a state intent on destroying the spiritual foundations that inspired it. I met with the artists who worked underground in defiance of the State; they looked to Jesus Christ, Author and Finisher of the faith for inspiration and consolation. These people are working on the cutting edge of some very real situations and they, in culturally diverse ways, offer their best to God who in turn had offered his best to them.

There is an emerging global community of Christian art makers struggling to put their faith into practice. Artists and thinkers have argued for and against certain ideas and approaches to the arts within the Church. Some talk of the celebratory "Cultural Mandate" approach—making "good art to the glory of God." I have heard those that talk about art as expression or an avenue of ministry in emotional and almost mystical terms. I have heard artists who think about art primarily as a communicative tool in the business of evangelism. There are people ready to defend each of these positions and raise questions about the other ones.

We all need each other, and should commit to exploring the tensions between celebration, expression, and communication. If the arts are important to the Church, as we say they are, then getting *artistes* out of their ivory towers and getting some of the other people out of their ideological and sectarian cul de sacs should be a priority.

We all need each other, quite possibly, so that we can learn to be supportive while learning how to disagree. How can we learn to "speak the truth in love," as Paul writes in Ephesians, if we restrict our conversation to a close circle of like-minded friends or, in the case of the "isolated artist," to the mirror on the bathroom wall? How can we possibly grow into maturity as artists, as thinkers, and as members of the Body of Christ? And yet this maturity is God's intention for us as believers. I believe that arguments and even disagreements serve their purpose in pushing each one of us to think clearly and deeply and work harder to the glory of God (see Prov. 27:17 and Heb. 10:24). Developing a community that is not afraid to risk exploration, dialogue, and even unanswered questions in the arts and culture will be essential if we, as Christian artists are going to have anything to say. And if we are going to have anything to say, now is the time to say it.

But why us? Why here? Why now? I hope to answer these questions. I begin with a quick-paced journey through the history of thought in Western culture, from the place of the ideal and absolutes in Greek and early Christian philosophy to the "deconstructing" of absolutes in postmodernism. From this overview we will explore the changing place of the artist in society.

In the next section I analyze some misunderstandings that prevent artists from thinking clearly and working towards doing their best, in their art and faith. This analysis will provide a framework for renewal of the individual and the community.

The final section is call for dialog and partnership between the United States and our sisters and brothers in the Majority World church. I end with an example of approaching

Scriptures for personal application, and to show how we must dig deeper in study to reap the harvest of ideas planted in God's Word.

There are a few terms and ideas the reader should be familiar with before getting into the book:

Aesthetics. The philosopher Immanuel Kant outlined a theory in which any object is appreciated for the pleasurable response given to the individual, which cannot be proven empirically, but can be shared.

Contextualization. The practice of declaring or depicting and living out the Gospel message in cultural forms and terms drawn predominantly from the frame of reference of those you are communicating with.

Deconstructionism. French postructionalist Jacques Derrida's theory of literary and social criticism that holds all literary and social constructs can be viewed as "texts" which can be analytically dismantled in order to lay bare the underlying presuppositions, biases, and contradictions.

Dualism. A splitting of reality into two primary elements or perceived planes, from the Platonic ideal (unseen)/copy of ideal (seen) and spiritual/material.

Empiricism. A theory that all knowledge is based on sense impressions alone.

Epistemology. The study of how we know things: how we come to know what we know.

Metanarrative. The traditions (religious and cultural) and philosophical system that undergirds a society's worldview and values. Seen as "the way things really are, everywhere" by its adherents/inhabitants.

Modernism. The theory that human progress will overcome all problems, through technological advance and the supremacy of reason

Multiculturalism. A movement mainly in art and education circles to expand our awareness and acceptance of cultural diversity.

Paradigm. A way of looking at reality, usually specific to a culture or group

Paradigm shift. A change in metanarratives as new information is introduced or old information is found to be mistaken.

Postmodern. A description of the era or society where the promise of modernism and its concmitant progressivism are abandoned or shown to be irrelevant.

Postmodernism. An philosophical construct in which values are reduced to personal interpretaion, without absolutes.

Rationalism. The theory that reason is in itself the definitive source of knowledge superior to and independent of sensory perception.

Relativism. The belief that all belief positions are relative and valid only for the individual or community holding them.

Romanticism. A nineteenth century movement inspired in part by the ideas of Kant, Fichte, and others that stressed the imagination as a key to our individual and social liberation and humanization. Accordingly, there was a great love for the exotic art of the past and from distant lands. There was also a celebration of the imaginative and the fantastic in the visual art and the poetry the Romantics produced. These Romantics included visual artists William Blake, Joseph Turner, Eugáene Delacroix, and Samuel Palmer, and the poets William Blake (again), Samuel Taylor Coleridge, William Wordsworth, and Percy Bysshe Shelley.

Scholasticism. A philosophical movement that drew upon Christian and classical thought to build a complete framework for thought and conduct.

Syncretism. The practice of blending disparate elements from differing religious or philosophical viewpoints to create an encompassing worldview.

ONE

Burning Down
the House

Because this age is post-Christian culturally, Christianity has lost its relevance. Being intrinsically bound to a decaying cultural pattern, it cannot extricate itself from the compromises it has engendered and the alliances by which it shaped the past. To say, therefore, that this age is post Christian culturally is a much more serious indictment of Christianity than the homiletic reminder that every age comes anew under God's judgment. The latter is only meaningful to the extent that Christianity really and positively acts as a leaven in any given cultural framework. But today, the structures of the world have changed from top to bottom and Christianity, it seems, has been left out of them.[2]

O UR culture is burning like a house on fire. Ideals we cherish are swept away, and layers of thought which have supported us are exposed and consumed. To some, this is a cleansing action, opening the way for a society where the norms are abolished and personal vision is the final arbiter;

2. Gabriel Vahanian, *The Death of God* (New York: G. Braziller, 1961), p. 139.

others see the sweeping changes as a denial of accepted truth, and wants to put out the fire—whatever the cost.

The burning (or decay, as Vahanian suggests) does offer hope: there is a chance for renewal. The first step towards renewal will be to examine the cultural history of the West.

I will outline some general historical periods for the reader in this survey. Keep in mind the dividing lines between different eras in history are generally gradual shifts in culture and thought. Decisive moments in science and philosophy, and critical thought in literature and sociology took years, even decades, to filter into the other disciplines.

This is a thumbnail sketch of the past two millennia of Western thought.[3] If the reader is unaware of the foundations of the late twentieth-century American metanarrative, and does not understand the unconscious conditioning behind fundamental daily decisions, knowing what is behind this cultural mindset is crucial for contributing to the renewal process.

THE PREMODERN ERA
GREEK FOUNDATIONS

THE Greeks established a philosophical base for the Western world that stood virtually unchallenged for fifteen centuries. The Platonic, Epicurean, Stoic, and Neoplatonic schools developed wide-ranging aspects of philosophy, ethics, education, sciences, and the arts in their indefatigable search for the meaning of our existence.

---

3. Comprehensive studies like Bertrand Russell's *History of Western Philosophy* (New York: Simon and Schuster, 1945), are invaluable resources for more in-depth study.

Many of the ideas and theories of these schools were formed as responses to the conflicting philosophical and social theories brought forth by earlier Greek philosophers. The central issues were: Did ultimate truth disclose itself to reason or did it emerge from evidence presented to the senses, and was the world one undivided reality or many realities? These issues defined the framework of the developing world view.

In response to this framework, Plato formulated the philosophy of ideal forms. Plato saw the world as a shadow or copy of the ideal; every straight line, every tangible object was only a pale copy of the absolutely real one that existed in the realm of ideal forms. Visible objects and ideal forms were of the same essence, but on different levels. His ideas fell on fertile ground; the political and moral results were seen in a culture that gained unity with little or no regard for the individual—the individual existed to serve the state, because the state reflected the "ideal" of civilzation. Not surprisingly, artists and imagemakers, those who worked at a "third remove" from ultimate reality, were looked upon unsympathetically by Plato.

The collapse of the Greek states after Alexander the Great resulted in a new look at the identity and importance of the individual. From this realization grew two distinct philosophies, expressed most fully in Epicureanism and Stoicism. Epicureanism—with its indifferent aspect grounded in blissful passivity—was widespread, but faded during the expansion of Christianity. Stoicism came closest to what would be considered Christian ideals, with its recognition of

the common brotherhood of man, and obedience to *Logos*—
an all-encompassing divine wisdom. The ascetic element of
Stoicism would later see fruit in the religious monastic
orders, but the narrow and harsh attitudes it engendered as
a system for the "few, the proud," prevented it from being
completely accepted by early Christian apologists.

The most enduring Greek influence came through the
Neoplatonic school of the second and third centuries, AD.
Their teachings, the last bastion of the ancient Greek world,
deeply affected the development of Western thinking. The
division between the eternal essence (the One/the Good), the
soul, and the visible world were the final step in the Greek
search for the ideal.

THE EARLY CHURCH

THE Fathers of the Church were steeped in the orthodox and
apocalyptic teachings of the Hebrew nation, but quick
expansion into the whole Greek world brought the need to
codify an intensely personal experience. The New Testament
and Apostolic writers all set their gospels and letters down in
the internationally accepted Greek language. As the Church
faced increased opposition and heretical doctrines abounded,
the Apologists looked to the secular philosophers for support
of their claims, a place of "common ground." By the time of
Augustine (354–430), Neoplatonic and Stoic ideas ran deep
in Church doctrine.

Augustine is the juncture of the synthesis of Greek philosophy and Christian apology. His intellectual journey

through classical Greek thought, the heretical Manichean school, the skeptical New Academy, the teachings of Ambrose, and the Neoplatonicist Victorinus brought him to the realization that his intellectual assent did not line up with his moral actions. His complete conversion to faith in Christ set him on a journey towards monastic life; his writings on the nature of God and man bore much of the weight of the sustained intellectual life of the Church during the dismantling of the Roman Empire—and subsequent building of the Holy Roman Empire.

As the Church assumed leadership of Mediterranean and European life from the Romans in the third century, it established a unified religious base of culture. The Crusades at the end of the Dark Ages solidified the boundaries of the culture. The Roman centers of learning were infused with new ideas from the Middle East and the Orient as scholars from the Eastern Church fled west with their collected texts. A key point was the rediscovery of the teachings of Aristotle, a student of Plato. His physics had been incorporated all along, but his metaphysical ideas were out of the mainstream of Greek thought, and were largely ignored until this time. Beginning with Jean Roscelin (1050–1112) and culminating in the writings of Thomas Aquinas (1225–1274), the Aristotlean model came to the fore in Scholasticism. The new ideas had a profound effect on subsequent philosophical and moral speculation, even when such speculation took place among the intellectuals in the emerging secular culture of the Renaissance era.

THE RENAISSANCE

WHILE the Scholastic thinkers attempted to frame Christianity within a context derived from Aristotle, the worlds of science and art were drawn closer by architect Fillippo Brunelleschi's (1377–1446) rediscovery of the mathematical principals of perspective. His studies on the Baptistry of the Cathedral in Florence, Italy brought the world of the artist closer to the world of the scientist, giving perception studies a concrete and repeatable base. As Renaissance artists utilized this new approach to space and form in their art work, they not only orchestrated the contents of the picture around a hypothesized vanishing point, they also suggested, by default, an implied viewer. The artist built a "point of view" into the artwork.

The revolutionary theories of Nicholas Copernicus (1473–1543) and Galileo Galilei (1564–1642), influenced by Brunelleschi's ideas and work, were reshaping fundamental aspects of the Western worldview. They raised questions about the world's motion and location in relation to other planets and the sun. The Church hierarchy took a dim view of these modern discoveries that called into question the picture of the cosmos framed by Roman theology.

Yet many of the objective thinkers in the Church were appalled by the lax morality, ecclesiastical power broking, and scholastic distortion of what were essentially simple truths about grace and justification. Desiderius Erasmus (1466–1536) led the way for those who protested from the position of Renaissance Humanism. Others broke completely with the Catholic Church through a reacquaintance with ideas about faith and justification gleaned from Scriptures. The Protestant reformers, aided in spreading their ideas by the new "movable type" print technology, made contributions to the tremendous spiritual, philosophical, scientific, and political paradigm shift taking place at that time. The radiant artwork of the High Renaissance artists such as Michelangelo can be traced to this flowering of culture and ideas. The Protestants revived Augustinian teachings about God's sovereignty in election of believers, freeing the fate of the soul from the actions of the priests and the efficacy of the sacraments.

The Roman Catholic Church launched a counter-reformation to address the abuses and laxity within the Church and the theological issues brought up by the Protestants. The Council of Trent (1545–1563) stressed reaffirming the distinctives of the Catholic Church's confession of faith. The Jesuit order, founded by Ignatius Loyola (1491–1556) during this time, placed great emphasis on missions and education, making a contribution to the philosophical worldview that formed the background for the thinking of Rene Descartes (1596–1650) and the political theories of Niccoláo Machiavelli (1469–1527).

THE MODERN ERA
THE BEGINNINGS OF MODERNITY

DESCARTES is considered to be the first modern philosopher because of his pursuit of an irreducible foundation upon which to build his ideas. That foundation was the thinking self, the mind set in opposition to the world of matter. Benedict de Spinoza (1632–1677) followed soon after, constructing a paradigm that had both monistic and pantheistic elements. According to his hypothesis, everything that exists and can be known about is an aspect of God. Mind and body are two aspects of the same thing, and can be understood rationally or scientifically. All that we do, think, or study is linked to and participates in the Mind of God. Controversial in his own day, Spinoza's ideas influenced later thinkers such as Georg Hegel (1770–1831) and the English Romantic poet Samuel Taylor Coleridge (1772–1834). Gottfried Leibniz (1646–1716) argued that the world was made up of an aggregate of substances or energy centers (monads), all chosen by God and set into preestablished harmonic patterns of coincidence.

Francis Bacon (1561–1626) is credited with launching the inductive method of investigation and analysis of ideas, facts, and truths. The investigator built up a "big picture" from carefully gathered "discrete bits." Bacon believed that it was possible for such investigation to be comprehensively systematized. He published an attack on the precritical 'idols' of allegiance to community values, subjective impression, linguistic imprecision, unchallenged scholastic opinion, and tradition, claiming they would get in the way of this new systematic method of arriving at knowledge.

John Locke (1632–1704), in his essay *An Enquiry Into Human Understanding*, built on Descartes' radical self-questioning and dismissed the premise that the mind contained prior innate ideas. Locke thought of the mind as a sheet of white paper upon which the world supplied much of the raw material that formed the basis for human thought and understanding. This more subjective/empirical approach to human knowing and understanding influenced the theories of George Berkeley (1685–1753), who stressed the role of perception in the comprehension of any form of reality. It also formed the basis for the radically skeptical theories of David Hume (1711–1776), who took his empirical approach to one of its logical conclusions: All truth was predicated upon sensory evidence alone; therefore, all historic precedents and theoretic projections concerning anything were at best probable and, at worst, hearsay.

Locke's moderate empiricism did not just apply to individuals. It formed the basis for a version of the "social contract." This was a form of enlightened voluntarism in which individual liberty and community values were bound together in a supportive relationship. Earlier theorists such as Thomas Hobbes (1588–1679) saw the social contract representing the subordination of the individual will to the collective good. Jean-Jacques Rousseau (1712–1778) used the same term to suggest the role of the state was not so much to govern as to express the will of the people.

The ancient philosophical questions and issues about individual values also found expression in another area of human concern. The ancient idealist values of Beauty, Truth, and Goodness were no longer hidden behind a veil of changing appearances. They were not the analog to some spiritual truth jealously guarded by the Mother Church. They now resided in the heart of the individual. This new individual self-awareness was a composite result of the different social and historical forces and new ideas that flourished during the Renaissance. The individual inherited the role of assigning value. They also inherited some of the fundamental problems and dualistic splits that traveled with these ideas from their ancient sources.

RATIONALISM AND ROMANTICISM

THE Enlightenment thinkers hoped to build a worldview based on rational, empirical, and material principles to derive an understanding of the nature and destiny of humanity without recourse to any kind of religious hypothesis. They emphasized the right to self-expression and human fulfillment, and opposed the Church for its metaphysics and intolerance. Their concerns for freedom prepared the way for the political revolutions in France and America. Thinkers such as Denis Diderot (1713–1784), Voltaire (1694–1778), and Julien La Mettrie (1709–1751) were associated with this school of thinking, as were the radical empiricist Hume and Immanuel Kant (1724–1804).

Kant, however, is more popularly associated with his critique of views of self and society derived from purely rational or empirical sources. According to Kant, ideas and evidences were made accessible and intelligible to the mind only with the forms supplied to them by that mind. The manner in which the individual comes to know things, with prior descriptive categories located in the individual's mind, reintroduced aspects of earlier philosophical forms of skepticism—this time directed at rationalist and empirical theories of knowledge. This skepticism, in turn, laid the groundwork for a form of subjective idealism, with a separate realm or category of *value*. Moral, spiritual, and artistic ideas fell into this category; the ideas were necessary to a culture and civilization, but slipped beyond the shaping, cognitive grasp of the knowing subject. Our recent ideas about "art for the sake of art" are rooted in Kantian suppositions about value and in the ideas of other Romantic thinkers who built a theory of artistic value based on *aesthesis*, or "sense impression." Artists and writers associated with the Romantic movement argued for the imagination as a necessary component in genuinely human thinking and knowing.

As much as the Romantic movement may have been shaped by Kant, it had a more definite beginning in the works of Rosseau. Deeply indebted to the French idea of *la sensibilité*—akin to sympathy, but emotionally explosive, with little room for reason—he brought in disdain for the conventions of society, from manners to morals. Rosseau attributed a kind of Edenic bliss to primitive and rural man, and a subsequent loss of innocence and resulting alienation that came with the development of life in the city. English poets Coleridge and Percy Bysshe Shelley (1792–1822) drew from examples of revolutionary and utopian social theories and experiments to forge a link between the liberated imagination, and the concept of political liberation. This particular link was rooted in Kantian theories of ultimate value, and refracted through Rational and Romantic theories about the human condition. Jeremy Bentham (1748–1832) and John Stuart Mill (1806–1873) believed that in the absence of credible metaphysical explanations, Truth and the Good were linked to whatever was eminently useful or made the most people happy.

PROGRESSIVISM

FOR Hegel, the role of the knowing subject who ascribed ultimate value was not a matter to be limited to the sensibility of the individual thinker. It was, in fact, a universal spirit, or *mind* that was moving the entire created order towards a zenith of ultimate resolution and perfection. Hegel described this progression as moving through a series of cycles, in which a *thesis* was countered by an *anti-thesis* that in turn led to a resulting *syn-thesis*.

It was a combination of presuppositions derived from both Kant and Hegel that undergirded much art theory of the modernist era. Thinkers and theorists saw Hegel's ideas about inevitable progress towards perfection played out in a society caught up in technological expansion and the industrial revolution; the results were truly revolutionary. If, in the shadow of Hegelian speculation, it was the job of individuals and communities to take their part in this cosmic progression towards ultimate value, then it would follow that anything that stood in the way of this progression was against the best interests of the human community.

While progressive ideas like Hegel's had held similar influence through the successive intellectual and cultural revolutions, several factors in the nineteenth century guaranteed the far reaching importance of these ideas for the twentieth century. Territorial aggression and contact with new ideas fueled the political arena. These factored into increased conflict, societal instability, and economic hardship as nations and states expanded their borders, made successful or disastrous alliances, and tried to shepherd their people through political advances or reversals. The sciences continued to explore new ground, especially in the areas of geology, biology and organic chemistry. The ancient ideas of evolution and species selection were revived and buttressed by the research in the work of Charles Darwin (1809–1882) and Alfred Wallace (1823–1913). Survival came to be seen as the purpose towards which nature worked.

Technology came to the fore in the nineteenth century as the techniques of mass production were refined. The development of enormous resources of power through the use of steam and, eventually, petroleum products and the combustion engine, gave advancing nations access to nearly unlimited opportunities for material growth and the accumulation of wealth. This growth was deemed useful, rational, and profitable by many, but to others it profoundly affected concepts of self and social relations. Historians, social theorists, and artists of the time saw technology as a dehumanizing influence, impinging upon the Edenic innocence and the life of the imagination. The increasing reliance on technology in the capitalist state was alienating, insofar as it caused many to labor but few to profit.

As the oppression of modern progressivism eclipsed its positive aspects, many decried those who used appeals to morality, truth and religion to keep the "masses" in line with society's push forward. Friedrich Nietzsche (1844–1900) postulated that it wasn't so much a "universal mind," or a collective impulse towards survival, but more a "universal will" that drove Western civilization. He dismissed traditional assertions of truth as veiled expressions of the *will to power,* and talked of a synthesis between the rational and the ecstatic, imaginative side of man as a way forward to social and cultural equilibrium. Nietzsche suggested that equilibrium lay beyond the conventional categories of good and evil.

All these ideas continued to carry forward the ancient, unresolved issues about truth and knowledge, casting them in historically and culturally specific forms. Martin Heidegger (1889–1976) and Jean-Paul Sartre (1805–1980), leaders of the new existential philosophy, found hope for truth and authenticity in the ancient philosophers who had not been corrupted by rationalism, or in the process of recognizing one's true self as removed from the world of causal relationships, conventional explanations, and moralities.

Attempts to align the values of a worker with his labor and a nation with her people produced the more radical stands against the capitalist strands of progressivism. Karl Marx (1818–1883) and Friedrich Engels (1820–1895) believed the state was the people, and the will of the people should be the will of the state. The extreme socialism formed in the early part of this century spawned the reverse ideal of the state as the people, with the "birthright" of a race (however ill-defined) foremost and in need of protection in the face of international threat.

Liberation, for both the disenfranchised proletariat of Marxism and the weakened race of fascism, was part of the utopian analog derived from Hegel's vision of ultimate spiritual perfection and Nietzche's expression of the "will to power." The task ahead was to no longer merely understand the world as refracted through this or that philosophical or social theory, but to work towards changing the world—by any means necessary.

TWO
Shaking the Foundation

THE fruit of critical speculation in the late nineteenth and early twentieth century was the drive for a "heaven on earth." This drive followed several paths—each bloody, yet each assured of its own "rightness." Racial and class myths were disguised in rational explanation, as were the authoritarian and totalitarian consequences of those myths.

As the results of progressivism waxed towards the hideous spectres of World War I and the October Revolution, scientific discoveries had already set the stage for the next great shift in self-understanding and a new view of reality. The world pictures that emerged with the theories of Albert Einstein (1879–1955), Werner Heisenberg (1901–1976), and others shook previously settled worldviews to the core, much as the discoveries during the Renaissance had done. The traditional picture of time, space, energy, and matter changed; so did the understanding of the relationship between the *knower* and the *known*. Theorists like Michael Polanyi (1891–1976) revived inquiries into the nature of knowing, especially as it applied to recent theories of scientific objectivity. Was it possible to examine phenomena purely, with no intervening or distorting influences? Was reality limited to what could be measured and described, dismissing all else as undemonstrable and therefore irrelevant? What role did individual bias and communal tradition play in the investigation into—and handling of—scientific data?

According to the newer philosophies, all man's understanding is based upon interpretation and context, not timeless, universal facts. The logical and scientific certainties used to sweep away the cobwebs of metaphysics and scholasticism began to splinter and fall apart under the new assaults on uncontested assumptions and agendas woven into the worldview. These critical analyses into the formation of distinct metanarratives carried Western thought into that amalgam of social and critical theories called postmodernism.

With the earlier worldview being turned upside down, any theories of "a good society" or social control built on the earlier worldviews had to undergo radical review. How were ideas of what is "reasonable" and "real" being translated into social practice? How were ideas of absolute or ultimate truth and authority being used to sanction a political process or practice? How was reality being represented, and what was the agenda of those doing the representing? It was here that the postmodernist thinkers and critical theorists raised the questions and concerns that have contributed so much to the current postmodern climate. It is necessary to remember that many of these questions were raised in the wake of social upheaval and catastrophes such as two World Wars, genocide, unfettered capital growth, and technological expansion. Many of these situations caused some of the postmodernist thinkers to pause before society's claim to "absolute truth."

Some theorists are intent upon unmasking agendas of social domination encoded in logical discourse. Others point out that the concept of what is normal and desirable in society is reinforced by patterns of restraint used to exclude and marginalize those who do not quite fit the picture. Others pointed out that the dominant myths of our culture are no longer guiding stars, but rather burnt out lights.

SCHOOLS OF POSTMODERN INQUIRY

JAQCUES Derrida (b. 1930) is known for his theories of *deconstructionism*. For the literary and cultural analyst, a wide range of social and cultural phenomena can be viewed as a form of "text," and the text can be taken apart, or broken into layers to reveal the biases and contradictions woven through the construction materials (language). There can be no final fixed meaning to such a text, as authorial intent and reader response are both at the mercy of the impurities and limitations of the medium. There is an unbridgeable gap between reality and its descriptions.

Michel Foucault (1926-1984) wrote that all descriptions and definitions of truth are enmeshed in the power structures of a society, determining what is effectively "real" for its constituents. The concept of truth that works for that particular society is produced and determined by "multiple forms of constraint." Foucault attributes the source of these constraining forms (education, prison, and definitions of mental illness, for example) to the shift towards modernization that occurred in the late seventeenth century. His questionable history of these containing and defining strategies should not blind the reader to his insights into the way the concept of truth is used by some.

Max Horkheimer (1895–1973) and Theodore Adorno (1903–1969), key figures in the Frankfurt School of critical theory, have written extensively on the social implications behind the notion of "pure" or "autonomous" reason. Reason as a controlling agent in the formation of a worldview is no more transcendent or universal than the spiritual ideals and dogmatic certainties it replaced. As the world shifts from being merely a dim reflection of eternal realities and becomes the raw material we apply "all reasonable means" to dominate, then how we see ourselves and society undergoes profound change. Horkheimer and Adorno's theories challenge the myth of reason's autonomy, and suggest that the liberating and humanizing intentions of the Enlightenment have given way to new forms of constraint and control. The result is alienation. Logical discourse functions as a new kind of prison, a prison that combines instrumental rationalism (our ideas of what makes sense is linked to what works), expanding technology, and a model of logical thinking and self-understanding as deluded and as unreal as anything it claimed to replace. What was intended for emancipation, the critics argue, has simply turned into a new form of oppression. Freedom within this oppression is merely a controlled, illusory form of freedom, rather like getting to choose which picture post cards you put on the prison cell wall. All concepts and descriptions of truth end up enslaved to what is currently deemed "real" or "desirable." The agendas of an expanding technological worldview end up guiding people as to what is to be considered "reasonable" thought and what is ultimately "true."

For Jean-François Lyotard, collective value systems are grounded in grand narratives designed to idealize the past or romanticize the future. Postmodernism is the product of distrust of the larger narratives that have guided Western culture. The two "master narratives" have been of origin and of emancipation. Cultures strived to preserve (or fight their way back to) an essentially primal golden age, or they have been catalyzed by the narrative of emancipation, moving forward into greater freedom. Both socialism and capitalism claimed to guide culture towards greater freedom and self-realization. The socialist vision of the future offered to free the proletariat from the realm of alienated labor. The free-market vision thought the interchange of conflicting interests and the unhindered flow of capital would be self-correcting as a social model, and would offer the greatest potential for freedom and self-realization for its members. Enlightened thinking and rationalism were seen as freedom from ignorance and superstition as mystical experience and religious faith had previously offered the individual emancipation from finitude and sin. Lyotard critiques the narratives and predicts their collapse. The postmodernist is outside or beyond the dominant guiding (yet exhausted) narratives that have shaped the values and goals of our culture.

IMAGE AND ART IN POSTMODERNISM

POSTMODERN critics detect traces of masked agendas, restraining forces, and exhausted stories in the illusory realm of pure simulation in the modern media-driven world. The Frankfurt School thought it sufficient to analyze the all embracing machinery of the "culture industry" which used pop media and the domesticated avant garde to mask its manipulative and alienating agenda. In the shadow of such an analysis, social theorist Herbert Marcuse (1898–1979) and art critic Clement Greenberg (1909–1994) postulated esthetic dimensions in which pure, abstract art would resist assimilation and make a revolutionary statement. Subsequent theories of Guy Debord (1931–1994) and Jean Baudrillard (b. 1929) took the analysis to new levels, describing an entire "society of the spectacle" in which the alienated spectator/consumer is plunged into an illusory realm of simulation.

Jean Baudrillard outlines of a descending order in which a simulated image begins by representing reality, then progressively distorts its representation of that reality until it no longer even hides the departure and disappearance of that reality but, in fact, has become a separate, self-contained "reality" of its own. He describes a society in which what is "real" is represented to us in mediated forms. These mediated forms, this representation, is all we know, or can know.

For some postmodernist thinkers all assertions of authority are little more than plays for power. But who wants to be in charge, and why? And what does that mean for the rest of us? Questions like these fan the flames of the postmodern dilemma, leading many to rethink the relationship of the individual to science, society, culture, language, and even self-awareness. The individual in the age of faith said "I believe in order to understand." The individual in the age of enlightenment said "I think, therefore I am." The postmodern self is told that all knowledge is personal (in terms of influences and biases) *and* that the very concept of the person is starting to unravel. Of course, some schools of postmodern thought seem vulnerable to their own deconstructive agendas.

A CRITIQUE OF POSTMODERNISM

THE postmodernist theorist attempts to unmask and dismantle the assumptions of privilege and universal validity that reinforce the dominant reality picture. But where does the theorist stand? From where do they launch their attack? If logical discourse is part of the mechanics of control, then logical analysis and description of the problem merely spread the disease while searching for the cure. If the "grand narrative" of emancipation no longer implicitly guides our culture as a whole, then what vision or goal is prompting the critic?

If there is nothing to be gained—like enlightenment, or freedom—then why bother? To admit a goal even faintly linked to an agenda of emancipation is to reinstate the mythical "grand narrative" even in the guise of postmodernist critique. If we are completely immersed as a society in an all embracing illusory image (as Baudrillard states), then at what point do analysis and criticism cease to be part of the same image? If the worldview under deconstruction is so all-embracing in its effect, then it is present even in the critique, whether we are critiquing logical discourse, "grand narrative," or the mega media "spectacle."

Some postmodernist thinkers dismiss the notion of a singular, unified central position as merely one option in a multi-cultural society (or as a disguised power play). They rush out to embrace the decentered plurality they feel represents genuine liberation from the controlling worldview. In doing so, they side with a marketplace that has learned to keep the chips in play by offering plurality and transience as options in a smorgasbord of choices. In effect, the decentered postmodernist experience is offered as a commodity. Marxist critic Terry Eagleton reminds us that the deconstruction of prior value systems serves the purposes of the business conglomerate as much as it does any academic theorist, and Fredric Jameson describes some elements of postmodern culture as little more than manifest symptoms of the "cultural logic of Late Capitalism."[4]

Theorists of cultural studies insist such political critiques do not examine ideas about the individual and society. These theorists analyze patterns of spending and consumption within the postmodern world of monopolized capitalism and see the patterns as keys to subculture identity, not as symptoms of passive alienation. Style becomes politics as groups on the margins of society struggle to keep their "street credibility" out of the hands of those who would imitate and commodify their style and attitude.[5]

4. John McGowan, *Postmodernism and Its Critics* (Ithaca, NY: Cornell University Press, 1991).
5. Angela McRobbie, *Postmodernism and Popular Culture* (New York: Routledge, 1994).

It is easy enough for the postmodernist thinkers and their detractors to snipe back and forth, accusing each other of adopting a privileged position and ignoring their own agendas and biases as they make their critique. However, this does not fully expose what I believe to be its primary area of vulnerability. This vulnerability is in the postmodernist claim to have broken free from the collective past. The kinds of questions about the nature of truth that surface throughout postmodernist writing go back to the foundations of our intellectual and cultural history.[6] As I pointed out in the first chapter, roughly the same issues were being debated by the competing schools of Greek philosophers just before the coming of Christ. Epistemological and moral relativists debated with idealists and empiricists about what could be known, and what the relationship was between the Good and the True. I have suggested that this complex body of issues has reasserted itself in various ways throughout the history of the West. Certain philosophical categories were discovered and used in order to systematize theological teaching. Ancient philosophical and cultural sources were periodically revisited by secular theorists (sometimes in reaction to overbearing ecclesiastical tradition), and this resulted in new cultural infusions which led to wide-ranging social and philosophical changes for that culture and for subsequent ones. Philosophical refinements and scientific breakthroughs contributed to the ongoing succession of paradigm shifts.

Perennial questions about the nature of reality and the relationship of that nature to our perceptions and representa-

6. Colin E Gunton, *The One, the Three and the Many: God, Creation and the Culture of Modernity,* (New York: Cambridge University Press, 1993).

tions resurface from age to age and, in fact, in different cultures. Some thinkers explore parallels between postmodern deconstructive analysis of reality and some schools of Buddhism.[7] One author suggests affinities between the postmodern mindset and that of the second-century Gnostics.[8] If these suggested parallels and affinities have any validity then this would mean that resources for a Christian response are close at hand. It was the apostle Paul who spoke of "deconstructing" the Gentile mindset (2 Cor. 10:4–5), and it was Paul who displayed a working acquaintance with both the skepticism of the philosophers, as well as an understanding of the social and political implications of such skepticism when he wrote to the church at Rome. Both John and Paul wrote to the young Christian communities about the teachers of those heretical ideas that flowered in the second century under the heading of Gnosticism.

I believe the postmodern line of inquiry has not been able to completely cut itself loose from premodern and modern patterns of thinking. However, as the Western worldview—including that of the Church—has been powerfully molded by those premodern and modern patterns, the question should be asked: Is there a way of reflecting on some of the issues the postmodern thinkers raise that will help Christians bear witness to truth with and through the arts? Just as the Renaissance in some ways prepared the ground for the

7. Steve Odin, "Derrida and the Decentered Universe of Ch'an/Zen Buddhism," and Dale S. Wright, "Tradition Beyond Modernity: Nishitani's Response to the Twentieth Century," in *Japan in Traditional and Postmodern Perspectives*, eds. Charles Wei Hsun Fu and Steven Heine (New York: State University of New York Press, 1995).

8. Ihab Hassan, "The New Gnosticism: Speculations On an Aspect of the Postmodern Mind," in *BOUNDARY 2: A Journal of Postmodern Literature*, Spring 1973.

Reformation, perhaps some aspects of postmodern thinking can clear the way for a fresh restatement of Christian ideas and concerns. If the impulses behind modern and post-modern thought resemble the idealism and radical skepticism of the ancient philosophers, early Church heretics, and some of the Oriental meditative traditions, then it may well be that an informed response to the postmodern mindset is already mapped out for us in the pages of the New Testament.[9]

9. Brian D Ingraffia, *Postmodern Theory and Biblical Theology* (New York: Cambridge University Press, 1995).

THREE
What Is Truth
(in Art)?

THE prevailing ideas about what is considered art in Europe and North America tend toward painting and sculpture (galleries, museums, and installations support this bias). But the cultural practices and creative disciplines that influence perceptions of who we are most often fall outside this narrow and self-serving scope. Postmodern inquiry would like to adjust the picture. Before looking at the postmodernist rewriting of *what* art is, I would like to posit *why* art is. What is the artist pursuing as he or she creates? I believe it is *truth*—as the artist understands it.

ART AS HISTORY

IN what I call the *Age of Faith*, the artist tried to communicate religious truth through art. From icons to cathedrals, altarpieces to tapestries, most creative endeavors were within the confines of religious devotion. Artmakers sought to communicate what they felt were established spiritual truths to a society of the faithful.

Next came the *Age of Observation,* with perceived reality depicted in art. Artists served the truth of observation and perception. As the general worldview of Western society changed and the understanding of reality and verifiable truth changed, artists concerned themselves with truth in what was perceived as *real.* Some of the spiritual verities receded, or were understood in new ways.

This gave way to the *Age of Expression.* Artists shifted from depicting the truth of the observed world to depicting the *act of perception.* Our self-understanding was changing and artists concerned themselves not only with outer truth, but inner truth as well. Some began to equate truth with personal authenticity, and this authenticity was of a kind that could not, or should not, be restrained by habits or strictures of social convention. Artists began to explore the uncensored unconscious, hoping for a greater vocabulary for their expression of personal truth. In their desire to shake the habitual and the secondhand, some moved beyond imagery and symbolism into abstract expressionism.

Others went further in their search for truth and personal liberation into what I call the *Age of Formalism,* an attempt to purify art of everything that was not art. Artists and critics insisted the only acceptable truth was truth *intrinsic* to the properties of the art object itself. To contemplate the object "for its own sake" was to arrive at the *truth* of art. Described as a triumph of form over content, some artists working in this way felt they were being true to art, issuing an implicitly revolutionary challenge to a culture awash in images, and giving some of this "art as art" a political edge.

This emphasis on form is a disastrously wrong turn. The search for truth through art has led to a dead end. We must dig deeper, into what was going on behind the art object.

ART IN HISTORY

INTELLECTUAL and technological revolutions profoundly impacted the arts and the relationship between artist and society. In the Enlightenment, artists found that subjective values and feelings attached to the imaginative ways of dealing with reality were driven inward, away from the harsh glare of the outer world of facts and analytical thought. The arts were pushed to the margins of culture. This marginalization distorted the artist's self-image and self- understanding, but they struggled through the cultural changes towards greater freedom of expression. Even as the artists moved in this new-found freedom, the general understanding of art and art history were being reshaped by the mainstream models of progress and development with intellectual and technological specialization.

The idea of pure, self-referring art that was self-*defining* amd self-*justifying* was part of the way the rational culture tried to shake off the past and progress towards a bright new future. Artwork, stripped of all reference to anything recognizable outside of itself, was considered a mirror reflecting back our search for personal authenticity. Objective goals were substituted for subjective values, present reason for past revelation, and personal truth for timeless truths collectively shared and maintained.

[handwritten margin note: Going against social convention]

But thinkers in a variety of disciplines are saying this progressive modernist worldview is itself in a profound crisis. The earlier era of faith gave way to scientific inquiry and philosophical introspection. This in turn blossomed into a full-blown "deconstructive" meltdown, as the introspection ate through to the very foundations of thought itself. The shock waves from this crisis are still being felt at the individual and cultural level.

MODERNITY UNRAVELS

THE modern worldview began to unravel in several ways. The intellectual and social changes following the invention of the printing press in Europe, the new manufacturing technologies of the eighteenth century, the expanded circulation of capital, and changing patterns of production and consumption all affected deeply held assumptions that were considered basic, unchangeable truth.

Today, truth is expressed in three relativisms:

Cultural relativism. What is true is established by the value system of a culture. If there is more than one culture, there is more than one absolute truth.

Ethical relativism. If the cultural norms of true, false, right, and wrong are linked to an underlying set of agendas and interests, then there are no guidelines outside of circumstance, situation, and feeling to work out what is truly moral, or morally true, in any given event.

Epistemological relativism. Scientific certainties give way to probability and uncertainty principles. Some of the methods of information gathering and analysis end up changing the information and the results of analysis; what is true about some phenomena changes by its dependancy upon how you investigate it. Light, for example, moves in waves when analyzed one way, and is made up of particles when analyzed another way. Pure objectivity is a myth. A scientific inquirer brings opinion, commitment, personal bias and the influence of tradition and community to bear upon the work being done.

Modern art has failed in its attempts to confront culture. Its progression, in a continual game of leapfrog, would sweep ahead of culture, only to find itself awash in a tide that quickly caught, then overtook, all its efforts. Every move calculated to shock was absorbed into the system and neutralized via reinterpretation or outdone in some other area of society. The dissolution of absolutes in culture, ethics, and science made moot all attempts to create art that would confront, shock, or challenge the viewer. At some point, there weren't any more conventions to break. *Is this not a point everyth' acts?*

Moving away from impacting present culture, the critics and interpreters of previous works began to be questioned as well. The version of art history that laid the foundation for modernism came to be seen as a particular aspect of that history, not an encompassing whole. Artists were and continue to be rediscovered. Artists and art movements who were dismissed or ignored for not fitting in with what was the dominant trend are now rehabilitated, looked at with fresh eyes. Postmodernism challenges our ideas of what is good art; it also raises questions about previous models of art analysis and aesthetic theory and the resulting "official" version of art history.

How has our way of looking at and understanding art been influenced? If truth and reason are not neutral and universal but represent particular interests, what hidden factors influence our analysis of art? What is the role of the art critic in shaping how the viewer looks at a piece of art?

Some theorists would like to deepen our awareness of the necessary role of galleries, museums, and critical traditions in influencing how we view what is considered art. Not only is the art object positioned in front of the viewer, but the viewer, through a variety of influences, is positioned in front of the object. Both the constructed object and the constructed audience are part of what analyst Pierre Bourdieu calls "the field of cultural production."[10]

In light of these theories, some thinkers are asking us to rethink the different *kinds* of cultural production and their relationships. If every critical position is a historical construct, and if every construct is linked in some way to an underlying agenda—economic, political, or philosophical—of the society in question, then surely the gaps between pop culture, mass culture, and high art culture begin to close, or at least demand deeper critical scrutiny. If such time-honored boundaries are now open to reevaluation, it may be the subversive complicity of the postmodern artist is a more effective way of making a statement than the anti-art statements of the modernist. In this new landscape the moral indignation of an anti-art statement like Marcel Duchamp's defaced

10. Pierre Bourdieu, *The Field of Cultural Production*, (New York: Columbia University Press, 1993).

Mona Lisa gives way to the deadpan irony of Andy Warhol's silk-screened *Mona Lisa*. Duchamp questioned cultural values in an era of social upheaval while Warhol questioned the sanctity and aura of the unique art object in an era of mass reproduction.

We must be careful not to lose sight of the value of past observations and questions in our rush to dismiss the world-view behind them. Let us also be aware of the value of critically rethinking aspects of our own cultural history and, in turn, our relationship to other cultures.

ETHNOGRAPHY VS. ART

OTHER cultures are finally beginning to be seen as truly *other* cultures. In the past, some cultural artifacts would end up in museums as raw ethnographic data. Trophies. If they were admitted as art it was because someone found avenues of expression in them that conformed to their idea of what was good art. However, all that is being turned upside down. Questions of artistic histories, value, language, and possible meanings are brought up by the postmodernist enquiry in our own culture. More questions also surface as Western artists, critics, and thinkers are exposed to the ways the arts work in other cultures. The arts, spirituality, and daily life are woven together in culturally distinct ways in many parts of the Developing World. The deconstructive and multicultural emphasis of some postmodernist thought offers valuable insight into unexamined Western assumptions about the nature and function of art and artmaking. It also addresses the potential for popular yet relevant art. Before we get too far into the postmodernist mindset and extol its value to the Christian artist, we must look at the broad implications of this worldview and where it falls short in providing a completely viable framework for the artist.

FOUR
Where Do We Go from Here?

RESIDENTS of this postmodern world surf channels, quote brand names, and think in sound bites. Views on issues and opinions are continually being assaulted, assuaged, and anaesthetized by shock DJs, erudite talk show hosts, political spin doctors, and media-savvy TV preachers. Printed media of every stripe, color, and persuasion attempt to pull our ideas and feelings in one direction or another. Many of the sounds and images washing over us mask their true intent by aspiring to documentary neutrality.

The apostle Paul warned Timothy that, in an era like this, the Church will be vulnerable:

> For the time will come when men will not put up with sound doctrine. Instead, to suit their own desires, they will gather around them a great number of teachers to say what their itching ears want to hear. (2 Tim. 4:3)

The stable foundations have been dismantled in this culture of free-floating signs and images, of circulating signifiers with no final resting place. The Good News is still *good news;* we have something to say that is beyond our culture and has a solid foundation. And for many, the selected sounds and images that fill them may be all they know—for them, the gospel may not only be *good* news, but *new* news.

THE PERILS OF CRITICISM

THERE are dangers in the unchallenged assumptions and practices of postmodernity, that much should be clear by now. The danger of this analysis is to imagine it places us outside or above the problems being addressed; modern and postmodern critics have not avoided this difficulty in critiquing the shortcomings of other systems or metanarratives. In the Church, when we talk about "the world," we often create an *us* and *them* situation and end up planting the seeds of all that we feel is wrong with the world in the soil of our own backyard. We understand there are aspects of the gospel that resolutely oppose the value system of our culture. The word of God is definitely *above* culture, in terms of what or who should have authority in our lives. However, we must remember that we are *within* culture, and our calling in Christ is to play our part in the redemption and transformation of individuals and cultures. I believe the recent history of the religious subculture teaches all too clearly that unless we are moving forward in seeking the genuine transformation of culture, then we are standing still and *it is transforming us.*

For our part, we must first examine our assumptions and practices. We need to be careful that our approaches to teachers, trends, and the Bible are not as superficial and as fragmented as the cultural environment of the people we claim we want to reach.

The Old Testament prophets challenged Israel again and again over its compromises and shifting allegiances. The prophets "deconstructed" the idolatrous systems the Israelites bought into and went on to challenge the social iniquities and injustices that occurred in the shadow of these disastrous alignments. The prophets spoke of a day when the nations would stream towards the mountain of the Lord and bring him due worship. Whether reading of the folly of Baal worship or the blindness of Greek philosophy, we find a pattern of challenge and confrontation, and in some cases redemption and transformation.

As we challenge the shifting mores of our own culture, keep in mind that the messianic and prophetic pretensions of the modernist fine artist were neutralized simply by being put on display. The work was assimilated into the very structure it tried to criticize. Unfortunately, this happens all too often when Christians speak out; they are effectively silenced when given a platform. Admittedly, we often play into the hands of our silencers by limiting our criticism to aspects of the cultural sphere that we feel directly offended by. I believe that we are being challenged to move beyond mere reaction into a deeply thought-out response. How else can we avoid the *accommodation* of our point of view?

The postmodernist's critique of the failure of modernism ends up in its own paralysis. As the subtitle of one book states, *After Deconstruction . . . What?* Heaven forbid that we should ever content ourselves with a "Christian" theory about postmodern culture. As the Buddhist *koan*, or proverb states, "The raft is not the shore."

FIVE
Keeping the Body in Mind

THE image of the "inspired" artist working on the fringes of society grew out of the Romantic era, when the marginalization of the imaginative and intuitive processes that occurred during the Enlightenment was elevated to the level of cultural myth. Western civilization now accepts the artist as a solitary figure, working out his or her personal vision in relative obscurity. The Christian artmaker must see this myth for what it is, and understand that no creative action takes place in a vacuum; culture's mores and attitudes are reflected or opposed in every piece of art.

The crucial matter for the artmaker is to decide *which set* of community values he or she is going to accept. One community is rooted in the dominant value systems of the the surrounding society (ancient idealism? critical deconstructionism?). Another community will claim to be guided by biblical values and Christian concerns. The choice becomes more complicated when the artist realizes that some people within the Christian community base their ideas about art and culture on an approach to Bible reading and interpretation that is as superficial and as fragmentary as the postmodern culture around them. I want to focus on the Church in this chapter, because the artmaker must remember that she is a member of the community of believers.

THE BREAD

> Then Jesus was led by the Spirit into the desert to be tempted by the devil. After fasting forty days and forty nights, he was hungry. The tempter came to him and said, "If you are the Son of God, tell these stones to become bread."
>
> Jesus answered, "It is written: 'Man does not live on bread alone, but on every word that comes from the mouth of God.' " (Matt. 4:1–4)

In Matthew's account of Jesus' temptation in the wilderness, the enemy's strategy was to raise doubts about Jesus' relationship with his Father, and also to question the validity of his mission. Jesus answered the attack by quoting from the book of Deuteronomy. Here is the context of his quote:

> Be careful to follow every command I am giving you today, so that you may live and increase and may enter and possess the land that the LORD promised on oath to your forefathers. Remember how the LORD your God led you all the way in the desert these forty years, to humble you and to test you in order to know what was in your heart, whether or not you would keep his commands. He humbled you, causing you to hunger and then feeding you with manna, which neither you nor your fathers had known, to teach you that man does not

live on bread alone but on every word that comes from the mouth of the LORD. Your clothes did not wear out and your feet did not swell during these forty years. Know then in your heart that as a man disciplines his son, so the LORD your God disciplines you.

Observe the commands of the LORD your God, walking in his ways and revering him. For the LORD your God is bringing you into a good land—a land with streams and pools of water, with springs flowing in the valleys and hills; a land with wheat and barley, vines and fig trees, pomegranates, olive oil and honey. . . . (Deut. 8:1–8)

This passage focuses on the faithful nature of God, who established a covenant with the community of Israel. This community broke faith with God, and continued to do so throughout the Old Testament accounts. Jesus knew that "bread alone" was not the answer to the problems caused by these repeated failures. Jesus was to offer himself to the Jews as the "true bread."

In the sixth chapter of John's Gospel, Jesus does some mighty works. He feeds a great crowd. He walks on water. John paints a picture of a powerful charismatic figurehead. The intention of the Galileans, according to John, is to make Jesus into a popular social leader. There is a marked echo of the temptation narrative, which does not appear in John's Gospel. If Jesus had demonstrated the power to turn stones to bread, then perhaps the poor in the land would have been fed. Perhaps this would be the first step to overturning the oppressive tax system and ultimately shattering the yoke of Roman imperialism. Jesus' response to the wilderness temptation and his extended remarks to the great crowd demonstrates that "bread alone" is no lasting solution to the community's problem. Jesus asked the crowds why they labored for bread that perishes. They replied that their ancestors ate bread in the desert, and went on to ask for a sign from Jesus to prove that he was a genuine leader—perhaps a new Moses. Jesus concluded by offering himself as living bread, the only hope for a restored covenant and a redeemed community. At this point, many in the crowd left in confusion and disgust. Jesus' abstruse talk of eating flesh and drinking blood alienated them. They sought material bread that perished, and pinned their hopes for salvation and social liberation on a powerful cultural memory, a memory destined to fail them. The crowds walked away from the only hope for true liberation, in stark contrast to the great multitude that followed Moses out of the bondage of Egypt (Exod. 12:38). Jesus turned to his disciples and asked if they would leave also. They remained, although they did not understand all that Jesus said to them.

These two "bread" stories speak to the heart of an artist's concerns with community. Both the wilderness temptation and the account of feeding the Galilean crowd give Jesus an opportunity to identify himself as the source of truth, and the true foundation for healing and restoration. Jesus knew that creating bread for himself during his temptation in the wilderness and creating more bread for the Galilean crowd would have undermined the work he had come to do. Jesus intended to offer his life as a foundation for a new covenant between God and his people. These biblical stories and images speak powerfully to the communal and personal dimensions of an artist's faith, and he or she cannot ignore them.

THE VINE

As Jesus taught the disciples during their last hours together, he turned to another metaphor for community relationships: the vine.

> I am the true vine, and my Father is the gardener. He cuts off every branch in me that bears no fruit, while every branch that does bear fruit he prunes so that it will be even more fruitful. You are already clean because of the word I have spoken to you. Remain in me, and I will remain in you. No branch can bear fruit by itself; it must remain in the vine. Neither can you bear fruit unless you remain in me.
>
> I am the vine; you are the branches. If a man remains in me and I in him, he will bear much fruit; apart from me you can do nothing. (John 15:1–6)

Networking and community relationships are a vital part of "remaining in Christ," and this "remaining" is an essential foundation for Christian artmaking. The idea of community goes against the myth of the isolated artist mentioned at the beginning of this chapter; suffice to say that the myth has no relation to biblical principles. I believe that artists working in the Church, giving support and service to one another, is an aspect of the gospel that sends a visible message to non-Christians of the power and grace of God. As the artist's vision is nurtured and revealed within the context of the Church (whether the artist's work be creative acts for the edification of the Body of Christ or works that are intended for more evangelistic settings), the intent behind the work will come through.

THE BODY

In Paul's second letter to the Corinthian church the net-working relationship in community was intended to be a source of comfort and stability to the church.

> Praise be to the God and Father of our Lord Jesus Christ, the Father of compassion and the God of all comfort, who comforts us in all our troubles, so that we can comfort those in any trouble with the comfort we ourselves have received from God. For just as the sufferings of Christ flow over into our lives, so also through Christ our comfort overflows. If we are distressed, it is for your comfort and salvation; if we are comforted, it is for your comfort, which produces in you patient endurance of the same sufferings we suffer. (2 Cor. 1:3–6)

Paul describes a model of mutual support that relies upon the metaphors of circulation. Consider the overall context of the Corinthian situation that Paul was addressing—one of hyperspirituality and mystical elitism. The comforting of God becomes a wellspring of empathic compassion for the Corinthian sisters and brothers. Characteristics of Christian art are empathic and compassionate identification with fellow believers, and identification with the world of the non-believing viewer and hearer. But there are things that stand in the way of fulfillment of this ideal.

THE BODY: IN PART(S)

THE Apostle Paul used the human body as a metaphor for the Church. He may have drawn upon the fable told by Menenius Agrippa in Plutarch's *Life of Coriolanus* in which Agrippa compared the body to the actions and interactions of the citizens of Rome and the Senate. According to his tale, the various body parts complained about the idleness of the stomach, which endured none of the hardship and labor of the other body parts. The stomach replied that it took in the food and then distributed the nourishment and resulting energy to other parts of the body. Agrippa went on to suggest that the Senate worked in a similar way, "digesting" their counsels and plans and distributing the resulting benefits to the citizens. Paul used the image of a body to talk about his idea of a healthy church and how silly it would be for various body parts to decide they had no need of each other. One body part cannot say to the other body part, "I have no need of you." All the parts work together in a coordinated effort to keep the entire body functional. Not only are all these body parts in a relationship of interdependence, but they are also vitally connected by the supply of blood and oxygen moving through them, "networking" them. When blood cannot get to a body part, that body part dies. Gangrene sets in.

Within this image of the body we have a clearer picture of the way all the parts need each other and are functionally interconnected. When an artist loses sight of their connectedness in a community, they are in danger of becoming ineffective as a limb, a body part. When an artist is not properly nourished in relationships with those different from themselves, they can perish spiritually. Today's Christian artists are in danger of falling prey to spiritual and intellectual gangrene. We can become like the dried up branches Jesus spoke of in his teaching on the vine. And when an artist loses sight of these related levels of connection, it damages their witness to a world that has already been impacted by contradictory and fragmentary images of individualism and freedom.

The biblical images of bread, vine, and body are meant to help provide an antidote. These and other biblical stories and teachings offer models of affirmation and freedom, even artistic and creative freedom, that are not bound to the value systems of this present age.

SIX

No Other Foundation

CHRISTIAN artists in the West face an uphill struggle in a Church that claims to be grounded in the Word and yet in many ways is culturally bound. These artists must learn to read and analyze Scripture, to distinguish between what are biblical concerns and what are merely human traditions sprinkled with biblical-sounding phrases. Artists must learn how to properly interpret biblical passages, so that they will not be ensnared by the misinterpretations of others.

Brothers, I could not address you as spiritual but as worldly—mere infants in Christ. I gave you milk, not solid food, for you were not yet ready for it. Indeed, you are still not ready. You are still worldly. For since there is jealousy and quarreling among you, are you not worldly? Are you not acting like mere men? For when one says, "I follow Paul," and another, "I follow Apollos," are you not mere men?

What, after all, is Apollos? And what is Paul? Only servants, through whom you came to believe—as the Lord has assigned to each his task. I planted the seed, Apollos watered it, but God made it grow. So neither he who plants nor he who waters is anything, but only God, who makes things grow. The man who plants and the man who waters have one purpose, and each will be rewarded according to his own labor. For we are God's fellow workers; you are God's field, God's building.

By the grace God has given me, I laid a foundation as an expert builder, and someone else is building on it. But each one should be careful how he builds. For no one can lay any foundation other than the one already laid, which is Jesus Christ. If any man builds on this foundation using gold, silver, costly stones, wood, hay or straw, his work will be shown for what it is, because the Day will bring it to light. It will be revealed with fire, and the fire will test the quality of each man's work. If what he has built survives, he will receive his reward. If it is burned up, he will suffer loss; he himself will be saved, but only as one escaping through the flames.

Don't you know that you yourselves are God's temple and that God's Spirit lives in you? If anyone destroys God's temple, God will destroy him; for God's temple is sacred, and you are that temple. (1 Cor. 3:1–17)

Earlier in this letter Paul wrote of a determination to stick to "Jesus Christ and him crucified" in opposition to the lofty spiritual pretensions of his readers. Paul challenges his readers to recognize their true condition as one of immaturity and carnality. In the section quoted above, Paul likens the congregation at Corinth to a building, and describes the grace of God revealed in a crucified Christ as the only foundation on which to build. He goes on to admonish the leaders and teachers at Corinth to build carefully on this foundation, in terms of how they exercise pastoral care and in terms of what they pass on to the Corinthian converts by way of teaching.

Paul states that it is possible to be sincere in one's own conversion and yet be sincerely deluded in what one communicates by way of spiritual teaching. Such delusion will result in a lifetime of building with highly combustible materials! Paul is careful to distinguish between the sincere but mistaken Corinthian teacher and the false apostle who comes in from the outside with a message that "defiles the temple" by attacking the very foundation upon which that temple is built.

Though Paul's words are directed to the teachers and leaders in the Corinthian church, some of the warnings and admonitions apply to today's situation. I believe Paul's words have something to say to Christian communicators and artists, as well as contemporary pastors, Bible teachers, missionaries, and theologians.

The tendency when examining this passage is to focus on buildings and building materials. The focus needs to be on the foundation that Paul talks about building on. The teachers at Corinth and their contemporaries were urged to build carefully upon the foundation of Jesus Christ and his work. The context suggests that structures based on personality cults and legalistic demands will go up in smoke.[11] This hopefully will be useful medicine for all who, at one time or another, have been haunted by fear or guilt because their artistic work doesn't explicitly evangelize or minister in the

11. I am indebted to Ron Julian's enlightening analysis of the text included in *Biblical Interpretation: A Common Sense Approach,* by David Crabtree, Jack Crabtree, and Ron Julian (Portland, Oreg.: McKenzie Study Center, 1991).

way that preacher *a, b,* or *c* said it should. In fact, diluting or distorting the expression of a God-given creativity in order to fit into *a, b,* or *c*'s preconceptions of what Christian art should do comes dangerously close to the eye service and men-pleasing Paul warns about elsewhere. It may well be that a landscape painted for the right reasons will be more durable, pleasing to God, and less "combustible" than an explicitly evangelistic piece of artwork undertaken for the wrong reasons.

THE REAL ISSUE

THE primary issue here is not about using art evangelistically. There is enough elsewhere in this book that speaks to the questions of art, evangelism, communication, and community. The real issue is: how do Christian artists understand the grace of God, and how does it affect what they do? An appeal to grace is in no way intended to sanction a completely personal, anarchic approach to what artists do with their talents. Getting back to 1 Corinthians, Paul speaks not only to the Judaizers and the personality cult builders when he draws out the implications of God's grace; he also addresses those who declare themselves free from all ethical and moral obligation. He advocates a balanced walk in which liberty in Christ and accountability to our sisters, brothers, and neighbors is complementary rather than contradictory elements.

Part of the balanced walk Paul advocates involves clarifying and thinking through what it means to use art, ministry, and evangelism in combination. Are there agreed-on definitions of these terms—singularly or in combination? Are these definitions built on a solid biblical worldview or on "what currently seems to work"? Part of the careful building on the foundation of "Christ and him crucified" involves being able to distinguish between the two. I hope this book will help the Christian community think more clearly and biblically about these issues. Artists must come to grips with learning how to read, understand, analyze, and apply the Bible in ways that do not compromise or distort the intentions of the author or the meaning of the text. It is not enough to go to the Bible and in its stories and parables find precedent and principle for creative endeavors. Christian artists need to ground their understanding of why they do what they do—their epistemology—in a clear and sober analysis of what Scripture teaches. If not, they will remain immature, "blown about by every wind of doctrine," and Christian art will be compromised by pragmatic agendas that have been dressed up in fine-sounding "spiritual" language.[12]

12. I highly recommend Gordon D. Fee and Douglas Stuart's *How to Study the Bible for All It Is Worth* (Grand Rapids: Zondervan, 1982).

SEVEN

A Jar of Dead Flies

MAKE no mistake about it, there is a history of artistic excellence in the Church. When looking at the work of Rembrandt, listening to the music of Bach, reading the allegories of Bunyan, or singing the hymns of Wesley, I know that artistic excellence and spiritual depth can go hand in hand. Great artistic work done in the name of Christ has sprung out of a variety of historical, cultural, and theological circumstances. While some lament the postmodernist threat to cultural values, there are others who are aggressively redeeming the time and are using this window of opportunity to make Christ-honoring art that speaks incisively to the modern and postmodern situation. I have come across scores of examples in America, Europe, and Asia; sculptors, painters, liturgists, performance artists, and writers who are working and thinking in ways that show how their creativity and faith in Christ incisively confront their culture.

Postmodernist theory is kind—at least as it pushes us to rethink our history and our relationship to other cultures. A tremendous window of opportunity is open for Christian artists from a variety of social and cultural backgrounds to have their work seen and heard. The artists working towards excellence in the context of the Church are somewhat of a minority; they labor in the shadow of a majority of Christian consumers and would-be artists who unthinkingly reflect negative aspects of postmodernist values.

There are many examples in the Christian subculture of poorly executed art propped up with appeals to the spirituality of the artist's intentions or, worse still, the Bible itself. This practice is dishonest and sets a disastrous precedent in terms of biblical interpretation; passages of Scripture are ripped from their context, twisted, and misapplied. The art-makers insulate themselves from any critical discussion of their work and from genuine growth in their skills.

I would like to address some of the rationalizations and Scripture-twisting that I have heard from different people who offer their talents and gifts to God. Let me preface it by going back into the Old Testament to look briefly at what God is asking of those who bring offerings.

> When anyone brings from the herd or flock a fellowship offering to the LORD to fulfill a special vow or as a freewill offering, it must be without defect or blemish to be acceptable. (Lev. 22:21)

> When you bring blind animals for sacrifice, is that not wrong? When you sacrifice crippled or diseased animals, is that not wrong? Try offering them to your governor! Would he be pleased with you? Would he accept you? says the LORD Almighty. (Mal. 1:8)

God's opinion on quality control in sacrifices and offerings should be read in light of other prophetic thunderings about the abundance of sacrifice being of no value when the Law is disregarded. Offerings are not a substitute for a broken and contrite heart. But God, who requires truth in the inward parts, is not going to let his people plead inner disposition and good intentions over and above a lackluster offering, whether it be diseased animals or second-rate art.

Of course, standards of what is good and bad in art undergo modification from age to age and culture to culture—artists are not to become slaves to a passing value system. Learning how to disentangle themselves from the system while remaining true to their chosen craft and gifts and relevant to their time and culture are tasks which should drive the Christian artist to his or her knees as well as back to the drawing board.

I know that some of what is offered in the guise of Christian art does not measure up to the stated level of commitment. It is like this passage from Ecclesiastes:

As dead flies give perfume a bad smell, so a little folly outweighs wisdom and honor. (Eccles. 10:1)

Ointment or perfume, designed to smell pleasant, is ruined by a small thing, a dead fly. So virtue, wisdom, and honor are ruined by only a little folly. (I didn't know the phrase "a fly in the ointment" had a biblical origin.) Substitute "Christian art" for perfume bottle, it begs the question: What are our dead flies?

Diff. between perfectionism & excellence

Bad art MEANS not learning from what he's called you to

THE TANGLED WEB

> But God chose the foolish things of the world to shame the
> wise; God chose the weak things of the world to shame the
> strong. (1 Cor. 1:27)

I HAVE heard this Scripture given as a justification for poorly
planned or poorly produced communication, the assumption
being that God is powerful enough to override a lackluster
attempt at art. It actually deals with the lack of desirable social
status among the membership of the Corinthian congregation. Many of them had little or no money, social position, or
political clout. Paul is pointing out that God is able to reach
out and witness to his glory with their testimony anyway. This
in no way justifies offering bad art to the glory of God any
more than it justifies a Christian heart surgeon approaching
delicate surgery unprepared because he knows that God can
heal. What God *can* do and what he *will* do are sometimes
two different things.

Consider God's desire for inward truth, his unacceptance
of lackluster sacrifice, his compassion and empathy for the
suffering. Arguing that God will bless bad art offered up in
the name of the Lord is dishonest and presumptuous. It pre-
sumes upon God's power as an abstract entity rather than as
an aspect of the revelation of his character. Further, it insults
the audience and offers a Pharisaic, spiritual-sounding rationale for dishonesty. If I criticize a work, I am obviously
judging or, worse still, manifesting a "spirit of negativity."
Some might argue that God will honor the purity of the
intention and forgive a less than good expression. Maybe. But

it is dangerous to make the idea the realm of the spirit and the execution of the idea the realm of the material.

> What good is it, my brothers, if a man claims to have faith but has no deeds? Can such faith save him? Suppose a brother or sister is without clothes and daily food. If one of you says to him, "Go, I wish you well; keep warm and well fed," but does nothing about his physical needs, what good is it? In the same way, faith by itself, if it is not accompanied by action, is dead.
> But someone will say, "You have faith; I have deeds."
> Show me your faith without deeds, and I will show you my faith by what I do. You believe that there is one God. Good! Even the demons believe that—and shudder.
> You foolish man, do you want evidence that faith without deeds is useless? (James 2:14–20)

Having a wonderful idea for an art project, even in the name of the Lord, is only fifty percent of the process. The execution of the idea is as important as the idea. One is not more spiritual than the other.

I heard author and former *Time* magazine senior correspondent David Aikman address this question of excellence in the arts He suggested that different fears were major stumbling blocks. Two that stood out were the fear of failure and rejection and the fear of hard work. It is natural to look for ways of avoiding failure and rejection, or at least minimizing the chance of them happening. We might draw faint comfort from the fact that Jesus himself suffered apparent failures, setbacks, and rejection, but it is still a prospect from which we we shrink back.

What about hard work? In the arts, as in any other profession, learning how to use the tools of the trade *can* be hard work. The artist must also study the history of a chosen art form and grapple with contemporary ideas about culture and its relation to his or her craft. Sadly, in many parts of the Church, artists are seen as lazy people. Fear and laziness are not held in too high regard as exemplary Christian character traits. The counter strategy of those who disapprove of Christian involvement in the arts has usually been to tar brush artistic pursuits as self-glorifying, carnal, and worldly. Even worse are the attempts at art by Christians who believe the tar brushers and, rather than learn their craft, try to bolster their lackluster efforts by relying on outwardly spiritual work and good promotion. It is all rather like the missionary who refused to learn the language of the people in his desired mission field because he had a perfectly good megaphone that carried his voice for miles around. If they could *hear* him, then he could *reach* them.

Let me close with an example from the ministry of Jesus. At the wedding at Cana recorded in the second chapter of John, Jesus turns some water into wine, and, judging from the conversations surrounding the wine tasting, the wine was more than adequate—in fact it was described as the best. By turning the water to wine, Jesus revealed some of the meaning of his upcoming public ministry, and also took an ordinary wedding feast and transformed it into a metaphor for the coming kingdom of God. A number of spiritual images can be drawn from the passage and woven into an artist's understanding of Jesus' purpose and mission, but they all radiate out from the words "you have saved the best till now." Jesus made good wine and proceeded from there into his teaching and public ministry, building on the foundation of potent metaphors like this one. The same is true for those of us in the arts. Jesus saw nothing wrong with providing vintage wine, both for the celebration and also for the bigger picture of the gospel. Taking the same approach of combining inspiration and materials, the artist can make art that is offered first to God, and then to his or her neighbor.

Now more than ever the artist needs to question if what he or she offers to God is going to be a pleasant-smelling sacrifice, like the spikenard that Mary anointed Jesus with in John chapter 12, or is it more like a perfume ruined with the dead flies of spiritual pretension? A pretension tragically evident in recent history by attempts to blackmail God into accepting second-best work through misquoting fragments of his own Word back to him!

EIGHT
Beautiful Feet
and/or Dirty Feet

How beautiful on the mountains are the feet of those who bring good news, who proclaim peace, who bring good tidings, who proclaim salvation, who say to Zion, "Your God reigns!" (Isa. 52:7)

THE thirteenth chapter of John's Gospel tells the account of Jesus' last meal with his disciples. Jesus takes a towel and a basin and begins to wash their feet. Peter protests loudly. Jesus reminds Peter and the other disciples that they are already clean because of their involvement with him and his word, but the foot washing was still necessary. The act was a picture of servant leadership and a model of how Jesus wanted the disciples to serve one another.

Christian communities throughout the history of the Church have found different ways to incorporate the practice of footwashing into their worship. Some have made it part of their communion service. Others have translated the act into a ritual of great pomp and dignity, far removed from its humble and practical beginnings.

In order to understand how the Isaiah passage and the foot washing story relate to Christian cultural workers and artists, some of the accounts where Jesus commissioned his disciples need to be reviewed. Jesus sent his disciples on foot from village to village to proclaim the Good News of the kingdom. In villages that did not welcome them the disciples were to "shake the dust from their feet." They were not tramping around in athletic shoes, or military boots, but some form of open-toed sandal. It is possible today to go into parts of the world—India, Africa, Southeast Asia—and the village streets are as hot and dusty as they were in first century Palestine. If all that is between you and the road you are sharing with goats, sheep, and chickens is a pair of sandals, then your feet are going to get dirty, fast!

The "beautiful feet" of Isaiah's proclamation and the "dirty feet" of John's Gospel are connected. This is especially true for Christian artists. Workers, craftsmen, and artists throughout the ages have used their creative gifts to bear witness to both the humanity and the majesty of Christ. They have used line, color, melody, and word to celebrate his life, from infancy, through adult ministry of miracle and teaching, to his final meal with his closest followers. They have celebrated his solitude in the garden, the agony of his death, and the triumph of his resurrection. The makers of icons in the early church created images of Christ for the faithful to contemplate the mystery of *God with us*. The medieval painters offered more realistic renderings of Biblical scenes, or recast gospel stories in images that reflected the life and times of medieval Europe. Christian artists at other times have dignified the landscape and portrait genres, using their gifts to celebrate aspects of God's creation. Still others have used their skills to try and portray the marginalized and suffering in ways that affirmed the humanity of their subjects while revealing Christ's depth of feeling towards them.

Looking at artistic expression woven through the history of the Church, the idea of the Christian artist has some validity and some precedent. The validity of "mission" in conjunction with the work of the artist can also be seen. What we react strongly to is the possibility of these ideas being used with any merit as we look at what fills the shelves and walls of bookstores today. We are wary of the concept of artists being propaganda merchants or sermon illustrators. Painting a picture is not the same as preaching a sermon. But we must remember that art, once it enters the public arena, ends up saying something.

ART AND AGENDA

THE waters can get a bit muddied here. The artist has something to say. Museums and galleries have a point to make by selecting one piece of art over another for display. Perhaps the critic will claim to discern a philosophical or political agenda in the work, or project one of his own onto the work's surface, influencing the viewer's perception of the work. A broad range of agendas have been represented through the arts, and not all the agendas have been representive of the interests and ideas of the artist. The museum rewrites our understanding of art history and, incidentally, our understanding of other cultures by *what* it chooses to display and what it says *about* the displays. Critics of all stripes shape public perception of artwork. Sometimes politics enter the picture. Artists and artwork are seized upon and reinterpreted in heated debates about public funding for the arts. Some artists become unwitting cultural ambassadors for the freedoms in our culture when their artwork is sent to be displayed in less-than-friendly political climates.

The interpretation of what constitues Christian art comes in similar ways. Within the religious subculture is a mindset that generates and reinforces mistakes in biblical interpretation; distorted theology is then used to justify certain approaches to art. These interpretive errors intersected with economic agendas to create the present cultural environment. I call the propagators of these errors the *clean-feet brigade*. These are the people who would like the Church to keep its feet clean; the brigade's method is to avoid getting dirty in the first place. Their favorite tool of persuasion is the Bible. Of course, they reinterpret it in order to slant the reading of it, much as some art critics and museum curators try to influence the reading of an art object or cultural exhibit.

When reading through the letters of the Apostle Paul, it is understood that he was tackling heresies that were troubling the minds of some converts in the infant churches. Some heretics were claiming to be purveyors of exotic mysteries and spiritual experiences. Paul reminded his readers that true spirituality and mystery was in the simplicity of Christ (1 Cor. 2:2; 2 Cor. 11:3). Some heretics were insisting that Jewish rules and regulations, such as dietary laws and circumcision, were important to the salvation of Gentile believers. Paul wrote to the congregation at Philippi that such people were "earthly minded," choosing to "glory in their shame;" their God was their belly, and as such they were "enemies of the Cross" (Phil. 3:18–19). Paul wrote to believers in Colossae and reminded them that all things were created through Jesus Christ and were reconciled to God by the blood of his Cross (Col. 1:10–22). Jesus was not simply one of a hierarchy of angels or spirit beings with whom the believers had to negotiate and to whom they had to be obedient in order to gain access to the invisible realms. Paul said people teaching such things talked in very cosmic, far-out terms, but they were only selling human tradition. He advised his readers to seek out the heavenly things and put their minds above, in Christ. This was in stark contrast to the hyperspiritual powerbrokers who Paul dismissed as carnal, deluded, and self-seeking.

Unfortunately, a lot of Paul's contrasts and contexts are not made available to us in the way the texts are sometimes preached, and some of Christianity is closer to the teachings of these heretical mystics who preyed on the early church. Is this world only a pale copy of some superspiritual realm of eternal forms (a return to Plato's ideas)? Perhaps the soul *is* a divine spark trapped in this body of clay. You may not hear it expressed in such bald terms, but that kind of disparagement of the visible realm and physical reality is often put forth as conservative Christianity—which of course it isn't. Is it any wonder that people with such a dim view of reality and such a suspicion of the physical realm sanction and churn out such bad art? It would be bad enough if it stopped there, but the clean-feet brigade like to confuse the issue further by accusing their critics of attempting to judge spiritual endeavors such as Christian art by the world's standards.

Given the terrible misuse of the biblical texts and the resulting misunderstandings of God's creation, I'm not sure that art, done under such a negative and oppressive influence, deserves to be called Christian art. The phrase "the world's standards" needs to be clearly defined if it is to be used in the pejorative. The commitment to such clarity will lead to a more exacting reading of art history and cultural theory. This is not the kind of work the clean-feet brigade is fond of.

The next line of appeal is to purity of intention. It may not look like great art, it is reasoned, but the value of the work needs to be spiritually discerned. If one is unable to see that well-intended and spiritually motivated art is, in fact, good art, then perhaps the viewer or critic is spiritually blinded and carnally minded. This appeal is usually followed by references to God using the artwork to "save" people as well as God using "foolish things of the world to shame the wise" (1 Cor 1:27).

God challenged Greek philosophical pretension, Roman imperial might, and the Pharisaic and priestly appeal to the Law and the temple with the gospel of Jesus Christ. The early church drew in slaves, women, tax gatherers, and others from the lower classes and the margins of society. It would be abusing both the context of the passage in 1 Corinthians and the intention of the author if such a passage were turned into a rationale for bad religious art.

Good
Heart + wisdom

Let us consider next the appeal to the numbers of people saved. "God is sovereign. People are sincere. This is what counts," the argument goes. The logical flaw here rests with the downplaying of the mediating agent. If all that mattered was sovereignty and sincerity with no attention to the bridge between God and man, it would render null and void the criticisms of the corrupt medieval church made by the reformers. Why not purchase indulgences to atone for sins? Why not make confession? Why should it matter if the communion cup is offered as a *channel* of saving grace, rather than a *reminder* of it? If God is sovereign, and a person sincere, then who's to say that God will not use the foolish things, including simple prayers to a few saints, to accomplish his ends in that person's life? We may balk at the oppressive and distorting approaches to faith that such religious practices present, but can we see that similar thinking is used to license bad and sentimental religious art?

What about the conversion factor? Jesus had harsh words for those who stressed conversion without adequately defining their terms, or while trying to conceal their agendas. Jesus denounced the Pharisees for traveling over land and sea in quest of a single convert, and then making them "twice [the] son of hell" that they were (Matt. 23:15).

Let's not mince words. If we attempt to justify bad religious art by pointing out that it is effective in converting people to a religious system that devalues creation, distrusts the physical realm, distorts the plain meaning of the Bible, and, in effect, destroys any foundation for true discipleship and obedience, then we're not merely mistaken. We are in active opposition to the gospel that Jesus and his early church preached.

ART, INCARNATION, AND EVANGELISM

IF we are going to appeal to the incarnation of Christ as a major influence on how we approach Christian artmaking, then we have to reckon with the historical and cultural aspects of God becoming a particular man at a particular time in a particular culture. These things are as important to a correct understanding of the incarnation as the spiritual and material aspects are.

> When we say of Jesus that He is of one substance with ourselves, sin apart, part of what we mean is that, like us, He was a particular human being, a determinate person, made what He was in part by His genes and the history and society of the world in which He came to be. Therefore no Christology is adequate which tries either to evade the material determinateness of Jesus or His Jewish particularity. Here we must reject out of hand any idealizing of Jesus, such as that which is found in modern theology, which in any way minimizes the importance of His Jewishness.[15]

Not only was the Word "made flesh," but it also "dwelt among us." To make genuinely Christian art, the artist must pay close attention to Jesus' communication method and its emphasis on parable, metaphor, and image. Jesus did not merely embroider systematic discourse with a few illustrations the way a modern communicator might. Nor was he

---

15. Colin E. Gunton, *Christ and Creation* (Grand Rapids: W.B. Eerdmans, 1992).

merely baiting the hook of the gospel with one or two juicy stories. Some stories he even left unexplained and open-ended; the story of the two sons in Luke 15 is an example. If the artist follows Jesus' method, he or she may find they are *not* having to join up all the dots for their audience, and do not feel obliged to explain the spiritual significance and meaning of everything they are doing.

If artists intend to make art that is specifically evangelistic, they must be open to the possibility that their art may be only a part of the process of evangelization. In the third chapter of 1 Corinthians, Paul writes about soil preparation, seed sowing, watering, and tending. Art may help fulfill one of those roles. It is unfortunate that some in the Church think that unless the artwork fills all these roles and then moves in for the kill/sale, it has failed to bear fruit. This is not true, and it is not fair to the Christian artist.

Art, even in an evangelistic context, should not shy away from the dark elements and jagged edges in biblical narratives and personal struggles. Dark deeds and attitudes are unflinchingly portrayed in the biblical narratives, and even darker feelings are honestly confessed in some of the Psalms. The artist also has "valleys of shadow" that he or she is passing, or has passed, through. While an artist may not rush to "embrace the shadow" and translate it into a viewable object, they should not deny its existence or ignore its role in drawing attention to the true light.

Finally, we will not confuse fidelity and fruit-bearing with immediate observable, measurable success. Rembrandt was hailed as one of our first Protestant artists, but a reading of his life reveals that, as he grew in spiritual depth, he fell out of public favor. It is also worth observing that his conversion and spiritual growth towards the end of his life never led him to abandon his evident skills in picture-making in favor of a more "spiritual" approach.

All these incarnational approaches have a high risk of dirty feet—which is why most of us avoid them. We also avoid them because of the casualty rate—we want to avoid the risk of a syncretistic blending of incompatible ideas, philosophies, and spiritual practices. But aren't we in danger of making equally dangerous compromises through apathy and conformity?

NINE
Overlapping
Circles

S ITTING on my bookshelf at home are two novels about
the samurai warrior code. In the first, *Samurai,* by Hisako
Matsubara, the samurai code is blindly adhered to and used
in a self-serving and ultimately destructive way. An old man
attempts to rebuild his family fortune by sending his young
adopted son to America to become involved in business. The
young man attempts to apply his samurai ethic in this strange
new world, only to find it outdated and irrelevant.
Meanwhile, the strain of his absence, combined with the further scheming of the old man, causes his marriage and family
to disintegrate.[13]

The Samurai, by Shusaku Endo, is set in the seventeenth
century. A samurai warrior travels to Mexico, Spain, and Italy
as an emissary of a Japanese lord seeking trade relations. An
ambitious Franciscan priest leads the samurai and his com-
panions throughout the three-year journey, acting as an
interpreter, but hoping to accomplish his own goal of

13. Hisako Matsubara, *Samurai* (New York: Times Books, 1980).

becoming bishop of Japan. The Japanese travelers undergo the expediency of baptism to further the chances of accomplishing their task, though they have no faith in the Catholic Savior. Through the story, the samurai quietly observes all the events; his true feelings come out near the end as he ponders on the image of an emaciated Christ on a cross—he is repulsed, yet haunted by the stories of a man who sided with the poor and the dispossessed, a man who was crushed and crucified by the rich and the powerful.[14]

If we were to treat these novels as two expanding circles—with rudimentary similarities, yet disparate in their core approaches—then their shared overlapping concern would be the critical deconstruction of the samurai ethos.

This business of expanding and overlapping cultural circles could also be applied to the situation we find ourselves in today. Western culture is undergoing a crisis in terms of its relationship with its own history and goals; it is also changing in relationship to other cultures. The overlapping circles of postmodernism and interculturalism reveal new ideas concerning the relativity and contingency of our own worldview or paradigm. Other cultural perspectives and worldviews are asserting themselves within the global village, and information technology has in many ways shrunk the world, bringing different stories and cultures closer together. All these factors have set the scene for another paradigm shift. The arts have been tremendously affected by this "reading between the lines" of our own worldview, and the comparison of it with other worldviews. Traditional art history, with its canons of

14. Shusaku Endo, *The Samurai*, (New York: New Directions, 1996).

taste and unquestioned assumptions about progress, has been turned upside down. New art histories are being written.

Our understanding of the arts and the artist was informed until recently by the governing paradigm of our culture. The artist, like experts of other disciplines, was a specialist working with a specialized language. However, users of this "art language" believed themselves to be increasingly at odds with the surrounding culture, though still driven by many of its underlying assumptions. These assumptions—about art, specialization, and autonomy—are behind much recent art history.

Some artists try to challenge the market-driven values and banality of our culture by making pure art. The art *form* refers to nothing outside of itself. The very austerity and simplicity of such artwork is offered as a challenge to a society saturated with images and agendas.

Some use their artwork to address a range of social and political concerns—the *content* of the work impels their creativity—but they still use the aura of the art event and the privileged space of the gallery or museum to display their socially concerned work.

And there are artists who bring together social questions with questions about the nature of art; the context of their work addresses these issues in combination. The relationship between artmaker, audience, event, interpretation, and responsibility are brought to the fore by the postmodern revolution in ideas.

ACROSS CULTURAL DIVIDES

QUESTIONS of art history's value, language, and possible meanings are not only opened up by the postmodernist enquiry in our own culture, they also surface as we are exposed to the way art functions in other cultures, where it maintains social and spiritual order and balance. Our relationship with other cultures is changing. In the book *Primitive Art in Civilized Places,*[15] Sally Price explores how objects from other cultures are displayed and explained to bolster our own interpretations of those cultures. She addresses instances in which such work has been displayed along with work by modern artists from our Western culture to suggest relationships and parallels that have more to do with particular ideas about art and artists than with how the cultural objects functioned in their original contexts.

Recent crosscultural exchange has opened doors of sharing and growth, with artmakers learning from each other and bringing new ideas and artistic enrichment to their respective cultures. The place of art in different cultures has also been examined more closely, and awareness of the spiritual and emotional importance of the arts in the Developing World has spurred First World artists to reexamine their motives for making art. In the Developing World, the observable meaning of a work is not sealed up in the surface of a static object, nor is it exclusively limited to the author's intention. A piece of art begins life with particular meaning, then different significances emerge as the public engages with it. The

15. Sally Price, *Primitive Art in Civilized Places* (Chicago: University of Chicago Press, 1989).

value of art in these cultures invites participatory dialogue, with different levels of meaning and significance arising from the dialogue.

Some Christian artists may welcome the overlap between the increased use of the arts in cross-cultural evangelism and the emerging postmodernist emphasis on interculturalism. Will these artists be ready for the crisis of values they might face following their exposure to other cultures? I believe some artists will look deeply into these issues and questions. Some will be challenged to rethink fundamental assumptions, as Endo's samurai did when confronted by the "weakness and foolishness of God" in the crucified Christ. And there will be those who, like the samurai in Matsubara's work, will cling to an obsolete worldview, condemned to irrelevance in a strange, new country.

Importance of
artsin developing world =
spurred 1st world artists
Re-evaluine their
motives & making art.

TEN
Masks and
Roots

SEVERAL years ago, while researching medieval mystery plays in York, England, I went to a local church production of a gospel musical written by Americans. The sincerity of the performers could not compensate for the transatlantic feel of the production. The next day I attended a High Anglican Church service in York Minster. The choir began to solemnly sing the Creed; within moments the words were swallowed up in echoes. The recitation became an experience without content, and the truth in the words was lost in the form and context of their delivery.

I heard about a similar instance when an American evangelical film was shown to a Japanese audience. The showing resulted in questions about the American lifestyle, the amount of leisure time and the abundance of home furnishings; there were no questions about the film's "real message."

The relationship between form and content in communication should be questioned when form modifies or even changes received content, like echoes emptying the recited creed of its message.

mEssAGES must bE conveyed through a pErsons culture

An image from gardening practices may help clarify this point. To move a delicate plant from one soil to another, one must first gently wrap the roots. The "roots" of the Gospel are the dynamic principles of incarnational living and communication that can be modeled and placed in many different cultural soils. Jesus is not a blonde European, or a Greek shepherd. He may have been depicted that way at certain times during the Church's missionary expansion. The Church has continually faced the problem of getting the roots of the gospel mixed up or confused with some of the soil that clings to it. Individuals tend to identify the gospel with the cultural form in which they received it. This is generally appropriate as a person seeks to make the gospel their own in terms of obeying it, and living it out daily in their cultural context. Problems arise when communicating the gospel across cultural lines; some of the cultural soil is often passed along as if it were part of the gospel's roots.

JESUS, THE INCARNATE TRUTH

KEEP in mind the roots of the gospel have one concrete, incarnational truth. The Word *became flesh*, and *lived among us* (John 1:14). There is an increasing emphasis on the concreteness and particularity of Jesus as a man with a culture and a history. This emphasis is an antidote to the syncretistic philosophies that want to locate "the hidden, cosmic Christ" at the heart of different religious systems. Within the Church, incarnational truth should lead believers to question the relationship between the message and methods of communicating that message.

I believe that, because God the Father reconciled the world to himself through the Son, the Church must think through the incarnational implications of communications across culture. The relevance of all this to our topic is that missions across cultures and artmaking need to be considered in the light of biblical teaching and example. Great artists and those who want to take a genuinely Christian approach to communication share the concerns of marrying material and ideas, form and content, medium and message, and the work and intended audience.

In February of 1989, I participated in a Christian Arts conference held in Bali, Indonesia with Christians from around the world. We explored many of the issues Christian artists face as they try to creatively express or communicate their faith in different traditional or contemporary cultural settings. In Bali, the spiritual and the material are subtly interwoven in ways that may seem strange to the modern Western mindset. The integrated nature of the Balinese culture and the pioneering work of the Church in Bali in redeeming and transforming aspects of that culture made the country a good choice for the arts conference.

THE CHURCH IN BALI

An example of this integration can be found in the work of the Reverend Wayan Mastra. While traveling in Europe, Mastra observed how Christians "European-ized" elements of the gospel. The way Europeans designed their churches began as a reflection of the culture around them; the Church took over pre-Christian festivals and "holy days" and re-purposed them into the celebratory days of Christmas, Epiphany, and Easter. Reverend Mastra returned to Bali and, in a similar way, "Balinized" the gospel. He built a church along traditional Balinese design principles, with a roof shaped like a mountain and no walls. This allowed the world of nature to be seen while preaching and when referred to in worship.

Artists within the church began to use traditional dance and drama to tell the story of Jesus Christ, creator and celebrator of the beautiful natural world, who nonetheless came among sinners to rescue them from sin and spiritual bondage. They made use of *Wayang Kulit* shadowplay, a beloved art form throughout large parts of Southeast Asia. The church workers and artmakers created new puppets and new stories in this artform—redeeming and transforming the form.

In the Balinese communion service the reclaiming and transforming of cultural elements was also markedly present. A traditional welcoming dance was done; the dancers entered with lit candles and used them to light other candles at the corners of a cross. A solo dancer with traditional mask bore witness to a new life in Christ, and gave an opportunity for all communicants to join in the dance. Tea, flowers and fruit were arranged on a white cross on the floor; the tea and fruit became communion elements. The cross was to remind us of the sacrifice of Christ, and the foot-washing ceremony and the communion were to remind us of our service one to another.

BALI REVISITED

AT a second arts conference in Bali in 1994, Kathleen Nicholls presented a paper on the artist as a "bridge builder." In learning how to build with chosen or appointed craft, she challenged attendees to examine their misuse of material, misunderstanding of culture, and shallow application of biblical principles. The theme of creative building was addressed throughout the conference.

Each day began with a worship session led by one of the representative "artistic medium" groups. The artists drew upon the qualities of their medium of expression for inspiring the celebration of and reflection upon the character of God or on a biblical theme. One group, led by sculptor Esther Augsburger, handed out lumps of wet clay. We worked the clay in our hands as she led us in reflection on its properties, steering us toward understanding the ways we shape our self-concept. This was contrasted with how God molds the obedient believer. On another occasion, the poetry group performed a composition based on Ezekiel's vision of the valley of dry bones. We built bridges from specific media to relevant themes.

We discussed examples of creativity in the Bible. We looked at how the prophet Nathan addressed David and his sin of adultery by telling a story about a poor farmer and a lamb. We discussed Jesus' story about the vineyard run by unrighteous tenants. Constantly we were reminded through these sessions of how images, metaphors, and narratives spoke to the whole person, yet addressed particular issues. We tried to imagine how such stories sounded to their original audiences, then worked on building bridges from these stories to our contemporary first world and majority world situations. Would we be able to import the methods used in biblical times? What kinds of metaphor and imagery would speak as incisively today? Lastly, We broke into groups and translated aspects of the stories—or images inspired by our reflections on the stories. Some worked with poetry or music, some with mime, drama, painting, or sculpture. We were all challenged in building a bridge between the theoretical understanding of a story or Biblical passage and the practical working with an artistic medium.

The group was encouraged, empowered, and challenged by ideas and disciplines outside each person's particular fields of study. I believe that these are the challenges needed today if Christian artists are to learn how to be effective bridge builders, rather than bridge burners. For instance, I learned a great deal about parables by trying to *write* one. The parable tellers in the Old and New Testaments balanced shrewd observation with pointed application. They were intimately acquainted with the life circumstances of their audiences and they were courageous in their confrontations and in dealing with the questions that subsequently came up. David was righteously angry at the villain of Nathan's story. The Pharisees were furious about Jesus' implication that *they* were the sitting tenants in a vineyard who thought they could take full control of it by killing the true owner's son.

Contemporary use of the parable can be seen in Bunyan's *Pilgrim's Progress*. Questions about Christian truth, charity and brotherhood echo through the great fictions of Tolstoy,

Dostoyevski, and Charles Dickens. Perennial issues of faith and doubt are elegantly dissected in the historical novels of the late Shusaku Endo. The wide acclaim and success of the stage version of Victor Hugo's *Les Miserables* speaks volumes about our hunger for stories in which we see at least partial reflections of our life's concerns. The parable, in both form and example, is rich with possibilities.

I believe that we can learn more about the biblical themes and stories by understanding not only how parables work, but how all the other symbols, metaphors and images play their part in the unfolding of the biblical drama. The New Testament authors drew upon the Old Testament imagery of sacrifices, the design and structure of the tabernacle, and the work of the priests to point to the reality of Jesus Christ. They talk about Israel's misadventures in the wilderness as an example for the young church at Corinth (see 1 Corinthians, chapter 10). In the book of Hebrews and in Paul's letter to the Galatians we find the authors using allegory to make their point about the inability of the Law and the sacrifices to truly justify. Jesus used a number of well-known Old Testament images to describe his person and work—the sacrificial lamb, the "son of man," the brazen serpent, and the true shepherd.

While seeking to be genuine bridge builders, should the Christian artist simply replicate familiar biblical imagery in contemporary media (a practice all too common in religious commerce)? Why not take a closer look at the *motivations* and *methods* of the parable tellers, instead of just slavishly reproducing their metaphors?

HISTORICAL CONTEXTS

When building bridges from theory to practice, word to image, and culture to culture, we should consider a few examples from our own spiritual and cultural history.

In chapter 13 of Acts, Paul spoke in the synagogue, using the Old Testament as the basis for his argument. In chapter 14, he spoke to a village of idolatrous nature worshippers, using the "general" covenant that God made with Noah, his descendants and all the animals and birds in Genesis chapter 9 as the basis for his appeal to the villagers. In Acts 15, Paul and Barnabas supplemented Peter's argument before the Jerusalem council on behalf of the Gentile believers by appealing to the evidence of the signs, wonders, and miracles that were occurring among these believers. In chapter 17, Paul reasoned with the Greeks in the marketplace, quoting their own poets and philosophers back to them as he prepared the ground for the gospel. In this four-chapter sweep Paul provides us with a dynamic model of contextually sensitive communication.

Another good example is the mystery play from medieval England. These plays provided a living book for the barely literate faithful by taking biblical stories from Genesis to the book of Acts (and one or two apocryphal and folk tradition sources). The plays created a dramatic cycle that entertained the audience while instructing them in matters of faith. Many of the dramas brought the stories down to earth by depicting the situations in contemporary styles and settings. People could recognize themselves among the medieval peasants and shepherds offered as contemporary analogs for the biblical characters. Everyone knew a "Noah's wife," who scolded and harangued her husband as he built the boat. Some could identify with—yet be amazed at—Joseph's lack of faith as he questioned Mary on the truth concerning her untimely pregnancy. Some pricked up their ears at the pointed social observation and commentary upon the respective fortunes of peasant and landowner offered by the shepherds as they watched their flocks just prior to the angelic visitation. These play cycles, eventually staged by trade and craft guilds, wove together moral exhortation, earthy humor and high drama to build a bridge into the lives of the audience.

ITALIAN RENAISSANCE

THE Italian Renaissance artists Fra Angelico (1400–1445), Donatello (1386–1486), Botticelli (1445–1510) , Leonardo Da Vinci (1452–1519), and Michelangelo (1475–1564) all approached their "Christian" subject matter in new ways. Use of pictorial perspective and to the revival of interest in ancient Greek and Roman philosophy and culture influenced how these artists went about their work. The harmoniously organized paintings and the radiant human forms depicted in them all spoke of an inner luminosity grounded in the ideas of Plato and the philosophers. The artists attempted to build a bridge from the majesty of their themes to the ideal values of the resurgent classical culture of the time.

NORTHERN EUROPEAN MASTERS

PIETER Breugel (d. 1569), Matthias Grunewald (d. 1528), Albrecht Dürer (1471-1528), and many other Northern

European painters dressed their biblical characters like European peasants, and depicted familiar gospel stories in settings contemporary to their time. They tried to use the pictorial, narrative, and symbolic conventions of their time to make genuinely Christian art. And as theologians, cultural historians and artists today point out, the work of these artists effectively built bridges from their cultural context to ours. In fact, as theologian Paul Tillich (1886–1965) suggested, Grunewald's Issenheim altar piece, with its horrifying image of the crucified, may speak as convincingly to our time—with world wars, holocausts, and death camps—as it did to its own.

ICONS

ANOTHER art form that builds a bridge from its context to ours is the Icon art form of the Orthodox church. The Icons were (and are) conceived as adjuncts to a worship and a liturgical experience that was patterned on the descriptions of chapter 4 of Revelation. The multimedia worship experience was intended to speak of the redemption and transformation of the senses. Not everyone, however, agreed that there was a place for such visual images in the church and its worship.

The Iconoclasts of the eighth and ninth centuries argued that it was wrong to try and depict the inexpressible via the image. They appealed to the biblical texts that forbade graven images. The early church fathers who argued in favor of the icons argued analogously from the incarnation. They spoke of Jesus as the image of God. The icon therefore (in the mind of the iconophile) not only gave an image for contemplative devotion, but also analogously "modeled" the relationship between the expressible and the inexpressible.

As artists learn to approach cultures, artifacts and texts with a balance of analytical and creative thinking, they hopefully can learn to discern and celebrate the evidences of God-given creativity, as well as the desire to communicate Christian truth in culturally appropriate terms. One can appreciate the artistry and be sympathetic with the intent while remaining critically alert to the shared philosophy and culture of the time. Some of the developing traditions within the Church might potentially dilute or change elements of the Christian message. A painter might laudably attempt to stress the humanity of Christ by depicting him as vulnerable child or infant in the arms of his mother. Such a picture might undergird the emerging popular and ecclesiastical traditions about his mother. The heroic figures of the Church, the saints, apostles, and even Christ himself may be portrayed not just as ideals, but as supreme examples to be followed to ensure one's place in God's kingdom.

Working through the early Church controversies concerning the use of images, the artist can gain insights that are relevant to present situations. As always, they should remember that all attempts at artistic and cross-cultural bridge building take place in the shadow of the bridge that God himself first built to us.

ELEVEN

The Life
of Signs

A T the first Bali arts conference I watched *Signs of Life,* a dramatic version of the Gospel of John produced by the Riding Lights Theatre Group from York, England. Evening noises pulsed around the Balinese "church without walls." Insects chirped, and the bell-like tones of a Gamelan orchestra drifted in from the performance of a welcoming dance in another building. As I watched the gospel unfold, I thought back to a trip I had taken to India, and was struck by the thought that John's Gospel could speak deeply into that culture—into *any* culture.

When I returned to America I read everything I could find on the Gospel that related in any way to the issues of art making and cross-cultural bridge building. I read material that explored the literary structure of the book and the social and cultural background of its first readers, and material that explored the different levels of reader response today, both in the First World and the Developing/Majority World. I read materials that exposed the tough political edge of John's writings, and devotional material written from an Asian perspective by a nun in a religious community on the banks of the Ganges. As I read the Gospel with fresh eyes and an open heart, I found many themes that drew upon the cultural history of Israel. At times these themes seemed to resonate in sympathy with the main stories and images, like the untouched but audible drone strings on Indian musical instruments. At other times I found images and patterns repeating in cycles throughout the clusters of stories, like repeating patterns and cycles in the music of the Balinese and Javanese Gamelan.

The more I read John's Gospel, I saw the author had taken his master's words "As the Father has sent me, I am sending you" (John 20:21) to heart, and had created a text every bit as complex and multileveled as the parables, signs, and teachings of Jesus. And, true to the incarnational nature of its subject, John's Gospel never floated off into airy disembodied speculation. The language, imagery and stories of the Gospel remained rooted in the cultural world of its original readers, while reaching out across space and time to invite us in the twentieth century to "come and see."

For the first century Hebrew readers, many of the great Old Testament metaphors for God's relationship with Israel would have been familiar. For others, possibly far removed from Palestine, the Gospel may have been almost like a courtroom drama, with a parade of witnesses for and against the accused. In every era and place there are people who see themselves reflected in the stories, whether outcast and margininalized, like the blind man or the adulterous woman, or caught at the center of some bureaucratic network like Nicodemus.

There was much material for rich and fertile reflection among the various cultural and social groups in John's time. I believe his Gospel speaks to artists about current possibilities within Christian art and communication.

Of course, there is nothing risk-free about the Gospel of John. Risks of faulty interpretation require caution and wisdom. They call for tough thinking and beautiful (but dirty) feet. No risks, in my opinion come close to the danger readers face when they sit back complacently and close their eyes, ears, and heart to the message, method and example of someone like John.

John's writings speak eloquently and accurately to a variety of cultural situations: the Palestinian and the Greco-Roman worlds of the first century , the postmodern Western and multicultural Developing worlds of the late twentieth century. To "come and see" what John has said to others, I believe we must begin with what John would say to us.

EXPENSIVE GESTURE?

In John's Gospel, we find an incident that resonates with one recorded in the seventh chapter of the Gospel of Luke. In Luke, Jesus was eating at the house of Simon the Pharisee. The meal was interrupted by a woman who paid homage to Jesus by washing his feet with her tears. The host of the meal, knowing something of the woman's character, inwardly questioned Jesus' judgment in allowing the woman to behave this way. Jesus told a parable about forgiveness of debts ("he who is forgiven much, loves much") in response to what he discerned in Simon's heart.

In chapter 12 of the Gospel of John it was Mary, the sister of Martha and Lazarus who anointed Jesus. At a dinner in Jesus' honor, she used an expensive perfume to anoint Jesus' feet, then wiped his feet with her hair. Judas who questioned the action, and accused her of making a pointless and expensive gesture. Mary's actions, in this context, were also open to misinterpretation—it was considered provocative for a woman to go about with unbound hair.

No one except Jesus seemed to grasp the significance of Mary's actions, and Jesus' explanation only deepened the mystery. He talked about being anointed for burial. This was a strange concept to be bringing up at a party thrown in honor of Lazarus, and at a time when there was widespread enthusiasm for Jesus among the people. The anointing was an extravagant as well as socially provocative gesture on Mary's part. Jesus' defense of her actions in the face of Judas's (and I suspect, the other disciples') indignation, only seemed to deepen the mystery.

Jesus placed a value on signs and sign making that had little to do with the price of the materials involved, and he seemed to show little regard for the social controversy and the lack of immediate graspability that came with the sign. Mary, in some ways, faced the problems that many sign makers and artists face today. They are told their work is an expensive luxury. They are told their work seems controversial, often for the sake of controversy, and they are told their work is obscure, for the sake of obscurity. When Jesus told the other celebrators to leave her alone, he upheld her dignity as a person and gave his support to the dignity of her gesture. He stated that this gesture of hers would be recalled wherever the gospel is told. Jesus reminds his audience—then and now—that images and symbols have value. And those who work with signs, metaphors and images *are* doing valuable work.

"THE POOR YOU ALWAYS HAVE WITH YOU"

JESUS did not leave Judas' concern about wasting a year's wages completely unanswered. Jesus' words "The poor you always have with you," have been interpreted in different ways throughout the history of the Church. Was Jesus suggesting that it was a waste of time for his followers to be involved in social issues? Was he pointing out that they would have more time for caring for the poor once he was gone? I believe Jesus was drawing upon the full import of Deuteronomy chapter 15, where the special seventh year, in which all debts would be canceled, is proclaimed. The laws set forth in that chapter also warn against being reluctant to make loans to those in need for fear of not being repaid. Just as the parable Jesus told Simon speaks of release from debt, so, too, did Jesus' words to Judas. Jesus was aware that he was being prepared for burial. He knew his death was going to be the basis of God's gracious offer of pardon to the sinner, with its cancellation of the "debt" of sin for all who put their trust in him. For Judas, the perfume Mary "wasted" represented a year's wages that could have been given to the poor. For Jesus,

Mary's gesture pointed symbolically to the upcoming events that would carry echoes of the "canceling of debts" that took place during the seventh year.

Price and value should not be confused in making art. Artistic gestures, even gestures that are hard to immediately understand, can have a place and value in God's scheme of things. It may well be, as seen in this incident, that some of the rationalizations against culture, arts, signs and symbols come more from a "Judas-like" mentality than a mindset renewed by the Holy Spirit.

TWELVE

The Well Is Deep, and You Have No Bucket

THE value of signs and images was seen in the story of Mary and her anointing of Jesus' feet. The incident where Jesus meets the Samaritan woman at Jacob's well (John 4:4–42) reveals a biblical model of the communication process, and recalls the ideas of form, content, and context.

ONE IN THREE, THREE IN ONE

WE need to examine this story in three contexts, and within these contexts discover parallels and distinctions in what is communicated, and why. The first context is the actual story and its three points of *respect, surprise,* and *discovery.* The second context is John's intended audience. Can we step into their shoes and respond to Old Testament allusions? Can we, from their perspective, be honest about whether or not they understood what was going on? The third context is today's artist's take on the story: What can be learned about Jesus' and John's methods of communication, and can this knowledge help the artist communicate more effectively?

THE EVENT

I'm going to tell the story, and glean from it the points of *respect, surprise* and *discovery*. Respect speaks of the shared understanding between Jesus and the person to whom he was communicating. Surprise comes in the way Jesus takes the dialogue to an unexpected place. Discovery shows the individual responding to what Jesus tells them about himself.

Jesus is traveling to Galilee and has to pass through Samaria. It is mid-afternoon when he reaches Jacob's well. A woman comes to draw water, and Jesus asks for a drink from her cup. She is surprised because what Jesus is asking is a breach of Jew/Samaritan relations, and would render him ceremonially impure. Jesus says that if she knew to whom she was talking to, she would be asking him for a drink (John 4:7–10).

Respect, surprise and self discovery. All three are evident in Jesus' interaction with the Samaritan woman. He begins a dialogue with the woman about water, while he is vulnerable and thirsty. This sets the stage for what he wants to say about living water. From here he will point back to himself as the resolution to the woman's moral dilemma *and* the historical tensions between Jew and Samaritan. Jesus creatively builds on a shared context (both he and the woman are thirsty). He shows the woman *respect*. He next introduces the element of *surprise* by puncturing a religious discussion with a barbed reference to her absent husband. Then he allows her to *dis-*

cover him as the true source of living water. She then leaves to communicate her discovery to her peers. When the disciples appear, they repeat the first mistake of the woman, taking his references to food literally. The disciples learn from Jesus that true food and drink is to be about the Father's unfinished business. He also comments on the harvest in the present tense, just as he had assured the woman that true spiritual worship was in the present tense.

TRUTH IN THE TELLING

In reading John carefully, I find a story that moves Jesus through sets of narrative and imagistic conventions that fulfill and profoundly subvert Jesus' native cultural and historical context. John's intended audience comprised those who may have misunderstood his Gospel as some people misunderstood Jesus, with superficial comprehension based on a literal "reading" of words and deeds. Some in this audience may have received insight into the meaning of what Jesus was doing. They may have seen through the veil of cultural symbols and images—helped by the way John tells the story—and grasped the truth about Christ. John's first audience was cosmopolitan, and he wrote a cosmopolitan gospel. For the Jew and the Jewish Christian, there were all kinds of emotional and cultural resonances as John told story after story in which Jesus sums up, personifies, embodies, and replaces distinctive elements of Judaism.

As they looked at John's take on the story, they would probably remember that three key figures of the Jewish faith—Isaac (represented by his servant), Jacob, and Moses (exiled from Egypt)—met their brides (Rebekkah, Rachel and

Zipporah) beside wells. John's telling shows Jesus fulfilling *and* transcending the Old Testament hero/leader model.

John frames this particular picture with some earlier remarks by John the Baptist. John the Baptist defends his status as a friend of the bridegroom (John 3:29). That chapter ends by pointing out the bridegroom has come, and *is* the Son. The Father has given all things into the Son's hand. In the story that follows, the Son travels and gets thirsty by a well near some property the patriarch Jacob gave to his son. While the thirsty Son sits at the well side, a woman comes along, and her entrance in some ways carries echoes of all the Old Testament narratives in which the heroes of the faith met their prospective marriage partners. Her lifestyle, however, is a shocking contrast to those virginal figures of the Old Testament narratives.

Here is where the plot thickens for John's audience. The three junctures in the story mapped out above translate into points of impact for this first audience. The shared *respect* context was Judaism. The *surprise* was the almost parodic bride figure. The *discovery* was of a bride who was not rejected, but purified by her groom, just as the Church was made of those redeemed and transformed by a Savior.

John's form decants these contents into a first century context. In doing so he works consciously to make the ingredients of respect, surprise and discovery available to his readers. Instead of merely a story about a confrontation, he tells a story that, by its very form, engages in confrontation. How will John's audience respond? Will they receive it gladly like the woman and the Samaritan villagers, or will they misunderstand it like the disciples?

WHERE DO WE GO FROM HERE?

WHAT about now? We read this story as sacred text filtered through layers of interpretation. Are we able to hear and receive the three aspects of confrontational communication I outlined earlier? Do the elements of respect, surprise, and discovery remain for today's audience? I believe they do.

In the actual encounter between Jesus and this woman, their shared frame of reference for *respect* was thirst. Based on what is said about her lifestyle, the woman was not only physically thirsty, but was thirsty for a genuine, lasting relationship.

Jesus *surprised* her by breaching traditional mores to get to the truth about her life. Her sarcastic response opened the door for Jesus to prove that he was indeed "greater than Father Jacob." His pointed inquiry into her personal life deepened her insight into who it was she was talking to, and resulted in her *discovery* of the truth of his lordship. It also set the stage for the evangelism of an entire Samaritan village.

In the first century reader's analysis, the shared respect context was Judaism. John's possible reference to Old Testament "wellside betrothal" imagery served to surprise in light of the woman's lifestyle. It also demonstrated that Samaritans—and afterwards, Gentiles—had less trouble approaching Jesus on his own terms than some Jews did. Samaritans and Gentiles, therefore, had their place in the New Israel, the Bride of Christ. That, too, was part of the surprise. Members of this congregation found plenty to reflect on and discover as they turned this story over in their minds. Was their situation as hopeless or as sinful as this Samaritan woman's prior to her meeting Christ? What of the disciples and their misunderstandings? How could one avoid their mistakes? True worship and the ingathering of the harvest were now present events instead of future promises. Was there a role for them to play?

How are we to truly hear this story? What does John's storytelling method say to us about *our* creative work?

Christians have a shared frame of reference in the Bible; in our context, it would be under the heading of respect. Surprise comes through reading a familiar text with new eyes, seeing how John's subtle narrative skills and use of cultural symbols bring a story and its central issues into the life situations of the reader. Discovery comes when a person considers what this story says about method and message.

John took material from a shared cultural context, and inverted its meaning to make a personal statement. It was a statement that invited response from the core of the reader, both in the first century and today. Are there equivalents to this in artist's creative work today? Can artists find ways of structuring their work so it draws upon the same kind of liberty and boldness that John exercised? Will new works engage audiences in similar dialogues?

THIRTEEN
Dropping Flowers
in a Basket

I N Bali during an altar call, those of us desiring to repent of something, or to pray, or to seek a deeper walk with the Lord, were asked to come forward and signal our intention by dropping a small flower into a wicker basket on the altar steps. As artists, we need to drop a few "flowers in a basket."

The parable of the prodigal son, recorded in chapter 15 of Luke, has been the basis for countless sermons on sin, repentance, and the longsuffering, gracious Father. The image of the returning prodigal has become deeply imprinted in our collective consciousness. Some have even alluded to this image when talking about the arts in contemporary society.

It is tempting to view the departure of the arts from the Church as a kind of prodigal son story. As Christendom was eclipsed by modernity and secularism, the unified order of art and faith so evident in the medieval church of Europe was torn asunder, and the arts eventually went their own way. Success and squandered riches were with the prodigal artist as he traveled to distant lands and cities. Now, lost in aspects of modern art that confuse and upset—in a sense, reduced to feeding pigs—the Church might even be ready to welcome a suitably repentant prodigal back.

Hold on to the images of a prodigal son and a flower of contrition dropped into a wicker basket, and prepare for some soul searching. What are some sins artists in the Church are called to repent of? I have outlined a few here.

Blaming other people, or "the world," or a conspiracy

When those "out in the world," or even sisters and brothers turn a critical eye on an artist's work, the artist is apt to become defensive. If their work is not accepted, it is because there is a "conspiracy to keep Christians out of the marketplace." If our work is criticized, it is because it is being evaluated in the wrong way, or measured by incorrect standards. All too often one rushes to demonize the critics and opponents to discredit their insights. In attempts to spiritualize the intent of their work, the artist insulates it from criticism. This is dishonest. Artists often try to hide the folly of bad work behind the foolishness of the cross. Remember that, according to Malachi 2:9, God sovereignly arranges for some of his priests and their message to be ridiculed and laughed at because of their disastrous compromises with the surrounding culture.

Being a stepchild of modernity/a postmodern consumer

The Christian artist needs to face up to his or her immersion in the modern world. "*Of* the world," or merely *in* it? I am not talking about abandoning motor cars, computers or rock music. The issue is not technology. It is a combination of worldview and attitude. Bigger and faster are not better. The artist needs to think through some of the assumptions of modernity and ask how those assumptions influence what they think effective Christian communication is. They must look at the rootless, free-floating, channel-surfing model of reality offered by some postmodernist theorists, and ask whether the reading and application of Scripture in the Christian life resembles the postmodernist's world in any way. I often run across stories that lead me to believe that the assumptions of modernity and the rootless channel-surfing mentality of postmodernity are woven into the mindset of the religious subculture.

Elitist attitudes about the supremacy of First World culture

A recent missions newsletter pointed out that a good deal of leadership in missions is now based in the Developing/Majority World. Leaders are emerging in social and cultural situations where creativity, communication, context and culture are interwoven in ways different from our modern and postmodern world. If artists can repent of the disastrous splits in their own thinking about communication, they might be of service to the new leadership serving the church throughout the world.

Stop misusing the Bible

The Scriptures were written in a particular cultural, historical, and personal context, yet their use goes far beyond authorial intent. The problem has been removing Scripture from *any* contextual mooring, reducing its interpretation to what we want it to be, whether partial truth or even false. Unlearning cultural habits and mindsets to the point where they are not impeding creativity and genuine communication begins with learning how to read our Bibles appropriately.

Idolizing instant success/instant results

Many artists and art critics within the Church might feel more comfortable with the idea of Christian art if it generated some measurable results in terms of conversions or sales of Christian merchandise. And it would be nice if the art was accessible, uncritical, and unchallenging. . . . The beloved hymn writer Isaac Watts wrote in a time when only Scripture passages set to music were considered suitable for worship. Watts never heard his hymns sung in church during his lifetime. What of Rembrandt, fallen from public favor, using his skills to depict biblical themes in a way that spoke more of personal experience than Italian influences? He died in obscurity and poverty.

How is today's Christian artist to truly understand the implications of stories like Watts' or Rembrandt's in an age when media ministries and mega churches lure them into confusing quantity of conversions with quality of conversion? How is an artist to truly weigh the spiritual implications of her/his gift and calling if they are surrounded by a mindset so locked in to the values of this passing age? Is the "Disneyfication" of Jesus any real surprise in a religious subculture that holds to these values? Thank goodness for the examples we have of dedicated Christian artists who went against the flow at the expense of acceptance, popularity and so on. Where are such dedicated artists today?

Many of the issues I have raised in these pages will require further reflection. Some call for reflection *and* prayer. Seek out the resources listed at the back of this book. Above all, reach out to one another as you make art that will carry us into the twenty-first century.

Radical

CODA

Am I Really Here, or Is it Only Art?

THE taped loop of Indah's words began, sampled fragments jumbling together into new patterns, new constellations. She laughed, told me I didn't understand, and then chided me for refusing a cigarette, "no smoke, no drink, no . . . ladies." The synthesized music began, with Indah's voice still murmuring beneath it, and I began to recite my account of going into Jakarta's late night streets and showing pictures of my baby daughter to the prostitutes I met there.

Questions nagged at the back of my thoughts . . . Was the backing tape loud enough? Why had I agreed to do this? Why did anyone think that work like this was suitable content for a worship service at a Christian Arts Conference? Did it give us pause for reflection, or enable us somehow to get a little closer to the plight of the outcasts of society, as someone had suggested? I wondered about what would be going through the mind of the African, Indian, and Filipino delegates as they listened. Was I just another First World visitor with his heart on his sleeve—but his passport, plane ticket and travelers checks kept close by for a quick escape? (The "emotional tourist" syndrome.) The piece ended, and the worship service moderator asked that everyone take a few moments to reflect on what they had just heard. After a short while, we all broke for tea.

People came and spoke to me about the piece. Everyone said they found the work moving. One person asked if I would be willing to send them a tape; they wanted to work out a dance or a mime based on the theme and content. One delegate wanted to know if there had been any "closure" with the girls—had I tried to talk to them about Christ. In a detached way, I heard myself defending my decision just to talk to the girls about my family and daughter, and how I felt that my encounter with them was simply one step in a communication process that might involve other Christians, other contexts.

I remember telling someone much later that it was easy enough to criticize Christians for wanting instant results or parroting superficial cliches, but Christian artists—myself included—were becoming adept in issue-dodging rhetoric, invoking the sanctity of art and the grace of God when confronted by hard and uncomfortable questions about the limits of accountability. Once, in Kansas City, an incensed truck driver assured me (and most of my audience) that what I was doing was "from the pits of hell." He wanted to take me aside for further exhortation about my lack of wisdom in talking about prostitution from the stage of a Christian coffee bar. The audience had politely endured my monotone readings over a variety of tape loops, but Indah's story and situation was the straw that broke the camel's back. "We didn't mind you talking about prostitutes . . . but did you have to tell us their *price?*" is one memorable quote that still haunts me.

The story is not over yet for any of us; there are many voices, many images still to be realized in the expanding community of Christian artists. Art, whatever form it takes, sometimes helps us to take a new look at what we call life. At other times life asks some hard questions about what we choose to call art.

APPENDIX ONE
The Gospel of John
A Study Project

I N the chapter "A Life of Signs," I looked at some aspects of communication in the Gospel of John. I have used the story in John, chapter 4, about the woman at the well in student study groups, and present a brief outline of that study for the reader.

Begin by reading aloud John 4:1–32. Try reading it from several translations.

Break into small groups and create word association trees. Decide on a word or phrase that sums up the most important aspect of the story, and write it on the center of a sheet of posterboard or on a chalkboard. Draw branches out from the center and place other words the group comes up with that are somehow linked or associated with the original word.

A tree might develop out of the following questions raised by the materials:

What is revealed in this story about Jesus as a person?

What is revealed about Jesus' methods of communication?

What do the cues in John's telling of the story suggest about the expectations of his original audience. Does he fulfill their expectations? Or confound them?

What else does John's Gospel tell us about the narrative and dramatic conventions of his time? Are these conventions applicable to our time?

From here I had the students generate performances based on their studies, group reflection, and word trees. In one instance we had everything from street theater to performance work that seemed to have little relationship to the accepted meaning of the original story, and more to do with a meditation on the process of communication through symbols. This exercise has been success in opening up a two way street between the gospel and art.

APPENDIX TWO

Lighting a Candle
Bringing Exploration of the Arts to Children

Train a child in the way he should go, and when he is old he will not turn from it. (Prov. 22:6)

WESTERN culture is increasingly image-based. Our children are growing up in a world that relies on pictures and sound to get its information, opinions, and messages across. Their worldview and thinking are being impacted and shaped by messages fed to them through a variety of media. Unfortunately, many children are in educational systems that are cutting back on arts programs, and opportunities for children to explore the arts hands-on are drying up. The child's world of color, sounds, and movement is increasingly linked to a world of marketing.

However, the proverb says it is better to light a candle than curse the darkness, so I am trying, through summer programs in the arts, to give children an opportunity to explore their creative gifts and learn to express themselves in a variety of artistic ways. It is, in part, a response to the disappearing arts emphasis in schools; I also see it as an important aspect of the

Church's overall life. It is a matter of stewardship over what God has entrusted to us in our children and their creativity; it is also a matter of discipleship. If the summer programs can plant the seeds of a truly biblical approach to creativity and culture at an early age, then children will have less to unlearn of the surrounding culture's distorted worldviews when they are older.

> His intent was that now, through the church, the manifold wisdom of God should be made known to the rulers and authorities in the heavenly realms. (Eph. 3:10)

Children are a part of God's family, and have their place in the local expression of the body of Christ. Their creativity is part of the contribution of the Church, and I believe we are called to help them make their contribution.

> It was he who gave some to be apostles, some to be prophets, some to be evangelists, and some to be pastors and teachers, to prepare God's people for works of service, so that the body of Christ may be built up until we all reach unity in the faith and in the knowledge of the Son of God and become mature, attaining to the whole measure of the fullness of Christ. Then we will no longer be infants, tossed back and forth by the waves, and blown here and there by every wind of teaching and by the cunning and craftiness of men in their deceitful scheming. Instead, speaking the truth in love, we will in all things grow up into him who is the Head, that is, Christ. From him the whole body, joined and held together by every supporting ligament, grows and builds itself up in love, as each part does its work. (Eph. 4:11–16)

Paul describes the role of the pastors and teachers in equipping the congregation for works of service. This involves creating an environment that encourages an informed, biblical response to the cultural trends and changes around us. Maturity and discernment are seen by the apostle as fundamental to the Church doing mission effectively.

Part of the Church's task should be to help the congregation understand the vital role the arts and media play in culture. There is value in creativity and the arts within the Church However, the "whole body" does not mean just adults learning to respond biblically to their surrounding culture. Children can also be taught to sift through the values of their cultural environment while learning about their God-given drive towards creativity. Adults should learn to understand that the creative expressions of children are works of service, and part of the process by which the whole body grows and builds itself up in love.

As children create, it enhances and deepens their appreciation of the gospel and the Bible. They can carry a deeper appreciation of drama, poetry, metaphor, melody, color and design with them into their own hearing of Scripture and their own worship. The Word of God comes alive for them.

Test everything. Hold on to the good. Avoid every kind of evil. (1 Thess. 5:21–22)

And this is my prayer: that your love may abound more and more in knowledge and depth of insight, so that you may be able to discern what is best and may be pure and blameless until the day of Christ, filled with the fruit of righteousness that comes through Jesus Christ—to the glory and praise of God. (Phil. 1:9–11)

Learn to test everything, and to hold fast to what is good. Our love should abound more and more in knowledge and depth of insight. The summer school of the arts is a valid and valuable way in which the growth and life of the Church is expressed.

Not that I have already obtained all this, or have already been made perfect, but I press on to take hold of that for which Christ Jesus took hold of me. (Phil. 3:12)

RESOURCES

Christians in the Arts Networking, Inc. (CAN)
PO Box 242
Arlington, MA 02174-0003
Philip Griffith, director

THIS organization has a global database, and is dedicated to networking Christian artists, arts groups, art festivals, conferences, college art departments, and related institutions. CAN is an invaluable resource for any Christian artmaker who would like to get connected with the goings-on in Christian art.

Fellowship of Artists in Cultural Evangelism (FACE)
1605 E Elizabeth Street
Pasadena, CA 91104
Gene and Mary Lou Totten, directors

FACE offers a wealth of arts and missions information, and runs an annual training school on a Navajo reservation. The group also organizes trips to Asia for crosscultural study in which students visit established artists, learn the traditional and contemporary art forms of the cultures, and share their creativity with their hosts.

BIBLIOGRAPHY

THIS is a list of resources for this book. It is not an unqualified endorsement of everything these authors say.

ART AND ART THEORY

Bourdieu, Pierre. *The Field of Cultural Production: Essays on Art and Literature.* New York: Columbia University Press, 1993.

Dillenberger, Jane. *Style and Content in Christian Art.* New York: Crossroad, 1986.

Dissanayake, Ellen. *What Is Art For?* Seattle: University of Washington Press, 1988.

———. *Homo Aestheticus: Where Art Comes From and Why.* New York: Free Press, 1992. Reprint, Seattle: University of Washington Press, 1995.

Dyrness, William A. *Christian Art in Asia.* Amsterdam: Rodopi, 1979.

Gasque, Laurel. "Voices of the New Heartland: Christian Art in Asia, Africa and Latin America." *Radix* 23:2 (Spring), 1995.

Lehmann, Arno. *Christian Art in Africa and Asia.* Saint Louis: Concordia Publishing House, 1969.

McEvilley, Thomas. *Art & Discontent: Theory at the Millennium.* Kingston, N.Y.: McPherson & Co., 1991.

———. *Art and Otherness: Crisis in Cultural Identity.* Kingston: Documentext/McPherson, 1992.

———. *The Exile's Return: Toward a Redefinition of Painting for the Post-Modern Era.* New York: Cambridge University Press, 1993.

————, and Denson, Roger. *Capacity: History, the World, and the Self in Contemporary Art and Criticism.* G and B Arts international, 1996. This last volume overlaps considerably with McEvilley's previous books. It's worth finding, however, for Denson's valuable commentary and critique.

Nicholls, Kathleen D. *Asian Arts and Christian Hope.* New Delhi: Select Books, 1983.

————, ed. *Voices At the Watering Places.* New Delhi: K. D. Nicholls, 1991.

Price, Sally. *Primitive Art in Civilized Places.* Chicago: University of Chicago Press, 1989.

Takenaka, Masao, and O'Grady, Ron. *The Bible Through Asian Eyes.* New Zealand: Pace Publishing, 1991.

Zolberg, Vera L. *Constructing a Sociology of the Arts.* Cambridge; New York: Cambridge University Press, 1990.

BIBLICAL STUDIES

Cassidy, Richard J. *John's Gospel in New Perspective: Christology and the Realities of Roman Power.* Maryknoll, N.Y.: Orbis Books, 1992.

Crabtree, David; Crabtree, Jack, and Julian, Ron. *Biblical Interpretation: A Common Sense Approach.* Eugene, Oreg.: McKenzie Study Center, 1991

Culpepper, R. Alan. *Anatomy of the Fourth Gospel: A Study in Literary Design.* Philadelphia: Fortress Press, 1983.

Fee, Gordon D., and Stuart, Douglas. *How to Study the Bible for All it's Worth : A Guide to Understanding the Bible.* Grand Rapids: Zondervan, 1982.

O'Day, Gail R. *Revelation in the Fourth Gospel: Narrative Mode and Theological Claim.* Philadelphia: Fortress Press, 1986.

Vandana, Sister. *Waters of fire.* Madras: Christian Literature Society, 1981. Reprint, Warwick, N.Y.: Amity House, 1988.

POSTMODERN & CULTURAL STUDIES

Connor, Steven. *Postmodernist Culture: An Introduction to Theories of the Contemporary.* NY: Basil Blackwell, 1989. Reprint, Oxford; Cambridge, Mass: Blackwell, 1997.

Gunton, Colin E. *The One, the Three, and the Many: God, Creation, and the Culture of Modernity.* Cambridge; New York: Cambridge University Press, 1993.

Hassan, Ihab. "The New Gnosticism: Speculations On an Aspect of the Postmodern Mind" *Boundary 2: A Journal of Postmodern Literature,* Spring 1973.

Ingraffia, Brian D. *Postmodern Theory and Biblical Theology: Vanquishing God's Shadow.* Cambridge; New York: Cambridge University Press, 1995.

Ingram, David, and Simon-Ingram, Julia, eds. *Critical Theory: The Essential Readings.* New York: Paragon House, 1992.

McGowan, John. *Postmodernism and its Critics.* Ithaca, N.Y.: Cornell University Press, 1991.

McRobbie, Angela. *Postmodernism and Popular Culture.* London; New York: Routledge, 1994.

Russell, Bertrand, *A History of Western Philosophy.* New York: Simon and Schuster, 1945.

Wei-hsun Fu, Charles, and Heine, Steven, eds. *Japan in Traditional and Postmodern Perspectives.* Albany, N.Y.: State University of New York Press, 1995.

OTHER REFERENCED WORKS

Endo, Shusaku. *The Samurai.* New York: Harper & Row; Kodansha International, 1982. Reprint, New York: Vintage Books, 1984; New York: New Directions, 1997.

Matsubara, Hisako. *Samurai.* New York: Times Books, 1980.

INDEX